Preface to the Third Edition

There is an interesting story surrounding the writing of this book. It occurred while I was an LFT in Canberra in 1977. I had just been told of a dream which one sister had. In this dream, Baba threatened to take His devotees and leave the planet if we did not do more work. This affected me greatly and for the next week I woke up worrying and wondering what I could do to stop Him. Then at dharmacakra, during Guru Puja, I heard Baba tell me to challenge the Indian High Commissioner to a public debate over the slanderous allegations which he was making about Baba and Ananda Marga (Baba was in prison at that time.) I felt fear about doing this, thinking that I would not be able to compete with the High Commissioner in a debate; however, I knew it was what Baba wanted and so I went ahead with my challenge.

The High Commissioner refused to debate with me, so I publicly announced that I would go on a hunger strike until he agreed to do so. The fast lasted for 108 days, during which time I camped in a tent outside the Indian High Commission building in Canberra. The fast received national and overseas media coverage and at times there were even tourist buses coming to visit me.

My continued presence outside the High Commission irritated and angered the High Commissioner and his anger came to a head when many Margiis joined me for a demonstration outside the High Commission after Baba was convicted. The High Commissioner lost his temper and tried to attack the Margiis, but police restrained him from doing so. Police then arrested three Margiis but they were acquitted after a video tape of the demonstration was used as evidence in court. The fast helped to highlight the injustices being faced by Baba and Ananda Marga in India, but it also gave me the inspiration to write this book.

During the protest fast my days were spent one-third in sadhana one-third in reading svadhyaya and thinking about Baba, and one third in sleep. I read an article by Baba on the qualities of Bhagavan which inspired me to type out a small book on the theme of Bhagavan using the Baba stories I had collected in a notebook. These were stories I had recorded during my first trip to India at the beginning of 1975. (Due to the tense political climate then I was unfortunately unable to see Baba.) Sometime later I found out that the carbon copy of the book I had given to the Sectorial Office, had been published. That became the first edition.

This second edition came out many years later and I added some of my personal experiences with Baba, particularly during the time I spent in jail. (With two other Margiis I was sentenced to 16 years imprisonment on trumped-up police charges of attempted murder and conspiracy to murder in the Hilton bombing frame-up. After we served seven years in prison, the Government released us with a pardon and awarded us a small amount of compensation for wrongful imprisonment. I have written about this in my book *Bombs, Bliss and Baba* (1998) also published by Better World Books.)

We have published this third edition simply because there are no more copies left. We have re-edited and updated the book and I have added a few more stories and Baba quotes and re-written some sections in the context of Baba's physical departure, ten years ago.

This book is purely an expression of the author's devotional sentiment and should only be read by others who have devotion for Shrii Shrii Anandamurti. If that devotional sentiment is lacking, the book may create a negative reaction, instead of inspiring the reader.

PREFACE 3

Please excuse the author's limitations in expression. I also apologize if the comments and statements made fail to inspire the reader or contradict their own beliefs. The Baba stories and Baba quotes are the main component of the book, indeed writing on the concept of Bhagavan is really just an excuse to indulge in devotional stories and uplifting quotes about, and by Baba.

Some of the stories are second or third hand, so forgive me if there are mistakes in the detail. However, I believe the spirit of the stories have been maintained and that is the most important thing.

"While doing our spiritual practices, while singing kiirtan and dancing we should remember the fact that all our spiritual practice is just to dance around Parama Purusa, lessening the length of radius, coming close to proximity with our ideological desideratum. We should always remember this fact "

All quotes in italics and separated from the text with lines are by Baba. I regret that it was not possible to give the sources of all these quotes.

The stories in this book have been collected from many sources, but I particularly acknowledge the contributions from the following Acaryas and Margiis:

Didi Anandamitra, Dada Abhidevananda, Dada Amitananda, the late Dada Asiimananda, Dada Bhadreshvarananda, Dada Bhaskarananda, Dada Cidgadananda, Acharya Dasharath, sister Giita, Dada Hari Shankar, Dada Jyotiprakashananda, Dada Nagina, Dada Parameshvarananda, Shankar Mukherjee, Dada Ratnadevananda, Dada Santoshananda, Dada Samanvayananda and Dada Vijayananda. I also relied on stories printed in the magazines: *Bodhi Kalpa*, *Pruijina Bharati*, *Pranam* and the books *The Flame That Burns Upwards* by Dada Jagadishvarananda, *One hundred and One Baba Stories* by Dada Shamitananda and *A Heartfelt Collection* by Dada Dhruvananda.

Thank you,
Narada Muni (March, 2000)

Bhagavan Anandamurti:
Stories About the Divine Qualities of Baba

A'charya Na'rada Muni

Better World Books
PO Box 177
Maleny, 4552 Qld.
Australia

Fourth Edition 2015
Third Edition 2001
Second Edition 1990
First Edition 1977

© *Paul Narada Alister*
paul_alister@yahoo.com.au

Cover Design: A'c. Narada Alister
Book Layout: Kamala Alister

To all those devotees
whose constant loving ideation
gives my beloved Baba
unspeakable pleasure
and happiness.

Contents

Preface to the Third Edition   1

Introduction   4

Aeshvarya • The Eight Occult Powers   9

Pratap • The Balance of Love   22

Yasha • A Mixed Reputation   29

Shrii • Beauty, Charm & Energy   45

Jinana • Knowledge   65

Vaeragya • Detachment   76

Conclusion • Surrender is the Final Word   86

Postscript • Baba's Departure   102

Appendix 1 • Secrets of Sadhana   109

Appendix 2 • Perfecting Sadhana   118

Introduction

> *"You cannot live without Parama Purusa and Parama Purusa cannot live without you. Bhagavan cannot live without Bhakta and Bhakta cannot live without Bhagavan. Bhakta has given attribution to Bhagavan."*

"Whenever Dharma is in decay and adharma flourishes in the world then I create Myself." These are the words that Lord Krsna spoke to Arjuna on the battlefield as recounted in *The Bhagavad Giita*. Krsna was the embodiment of Taraka Brahma and so when He said "I create Myself", He meant that Taraka Brahma will manifest in a human body. This physical body of His is the highest evolved body in the Universe and is His *Mahasambhuti* (Maha means "great" and Sambhuti means "created being" so Mahasambhuti means the highest evolved being.)

Mahasambhuti has been given many different names such *Mahapurusa* (Great Consciousness); *Mahakaula* (the one who has raised His kulakundalinii to the Sahasrara Cakra and can also do the same to others at will); *Mahasadvipra* (the one who creates Sadvipras—the

Lord of Sadvipras); *Mahadeva* (Lord of Lords); *Sadguru* (the True Guru-the highest level of Guru); *Tantrikeshvar* (God of the Tantriks) and *Bhagavan*. These are only a few examples as there have been many more names given to *Mahasambhuti* but it is the meaning of Bhagavan that I want to discuss and show through a few stories, how Shrii Shrii Anandamurtiji is Bhagavan.

In English, the word Bhagavan is translated simply as God. The title *Bhagavad Giita* means the song (*giita*) sung by the Lord or Bhagavan, who was then known as Shrii Krsna.

Bhagavan means He who possesses Bhag and Bhag consists of six qualities: Aeshvarya, Pratapa, Yash, Shrii, Jinana and Aeshvarya, It is sometimes said that the second quality of Bhagavan is Viirya which means potentiality and power. However, since I have an article written by Baba which state that Pratap is the second quality, I am not going to discuss Viirya as one of the six qualities of Bhagavan.

> *"Taraka Brahma calls everyone towards Himself:*
> *'Come on, come to Me. I have come here for you only.*
> *I am verily yours. Come and surrender to Me without*
> *hesitation. I will take care of your future.'"*

Following is the article I am referring to. This is taken from old typed notes which say, "Synopsis of a discourse given by Shrii Shrii Anandamurtijii at Nagpur."

Whose Directions are to be Obeyed?

Whose directions are to be obeyed? One should always follow and observe Dharma. Dharma and injunctions of God are one and the same. Dharma will not teach temporal difference. It is full of kindness, for everyone belongs to it; no one is away from it. Therefore, Dharma will not teach differences. It will not teach distinctions of high and low, it will not teach untouchability, it will, instead, teach fraternity.

Why is it so? Because you hear the voice of Dharma from God Himself.

What is *Bhagvan*? What is the meaning of *Srimad Bhagavat Gita*? *Ja Bhagavat Sa Gita*--that is *Bhagavat Gita* which has been sung by Bhagavan. *Bhagvata* means "by Bhagvan." Now, let us try to know what Bhagvan is. Everyone knows Bhagvan who is called God in English and *Khuda* in Urdu. He is called Allah. There are many names for Him. But what does Bhagvan mean? Bhagvan is He who posses *Bhag*. In the spiritual world, Bhag consists of six qualities. The combination of these qualities is known as Bhag. These qualities are *Aeshvarya, Pratap, Yasha, Shrii, Jinana* and *Vaeragya*.

Aeshvarya: *Anima, Mahima, Laghima, Iishitva, Vashitva, Prapti* and *Prakamaya* [and *Antarayamitva*]--they are all called Aeshvarya. It also means an occult power. This one gets through the regular practice of sadhana. One who possesses these quality is called Iishvara. But Iishvara is not Bhagvan. Bhagvan needs five other qualities also.

Pratap: Bhagvan has this quality. This is why He loves us and at the same time punishes us for our evil doings. Love alone will spoil a child. So also punishment or beating. Only He is the true Guru who rules over and loves his disciples.

One who only scolds is not a Guru but your enemy. He also who only loves.

Yasha means reputation. When Parama Purusa comes into the world in a physical form He will have staunch supporters on the one side and bitter enemies on the other. He can be identified by this phenomenon alone. On His arrival, the world is polarized; there is no one in between. There is no neutral. There will be both positive reputation (Yasha) and negative (*Apayash*) for Him.

Today, there are still many persons who are either the supporters of Lord Shiva and Lord Krishna or their opponents. It is so because of the polarization of the world by these great personalities.

Shrii: It means charm, attraction. This word is made of "sh", the acoustic route of *Raja Guna* (mutative principle.). This principle enables a man to work for it is an activating force. Ra is the acoustic root of energy (*bala*). These two letters together mean the preparedness of the mutative action and energy to perform action. There are many persons who have the energy but do not want to work; they are lethargic. But there are also persons who wok hard even if they do not have energy. There are persons who die working. This is very good. But better would be to work even while dying.

Jinana: Suppose there is an MA in Sanskrit. He has worked as a lawyer for 25 years after obtaining the MA degree. If you ask him after so many years, he cannot tell you anything. If an MA in Chemistry works as a clerk for 25 yeas, he will not be able to tell you about the formula for sodium bicarbonate.

Therefore, what they had learnt is not real knowledge. The real knowledge is the subjectivisation of external objectivity. In case of knowledge, there is a link between them which is called knowledge. Now, the subjectivisation of external objectivity means absorption of object.

There may be a defect in the knower of known. There may be defect in the medium through which we obtain knowledge. A patient of jaundice, due to a defect in the eye, will see everything as yellow color. He will claim a white and call out that with his own eyes. One cannot see an object correctly if light is not properly radiating from it. Such an object will present a distorted shape of itself to the eyes. You then can not see exactly what you should.

Real knowledge is attainable only when the knower and the known become one and the medium merges into this unity.

The pundits say that real knowledge is *Atma Jinana* (self knowledge). No other knowledge is real knowledge.

Vaeragya means that you are with the object, but uninfluenced by it. Such a state of mind really means Vaeragya. You have to live in this world but remain unattached to it. You do not have to leave your family or home to go to the forest for Vaeragya. Vaeragya Sadhana is possible even while living with the family and fulfilling all family responsibility. This sadhana is never possible in the Himalayan caves. Ananda

Marga avadhutas will also have to serve society while living in it. When you live close to an object you do not think much about it. But you do so when you are far away from it. The father may not think much about his son living with him but if the son goes far away, he always remembers him and waits for his return. Thus, one who runs away from the object will more and more come in its grip.

1
Aeshvarya:
The Eight Occult Powers

This quality is the combination of the eight powers or *siddhis* which are:

Anima—The power to become small in size or to view microscopic objects in full detail.

Mahima—The power to expand in size or space or to view the whole universe.

Laghima—The power to offset the force of gravity or to make one's body lighter than air.

Iishvitva—The power to control all creatures and elements such as the wind, rain and snow.

Prapti—The power to have or to create whatever one desires and to transport oneself anywhere.

Prakamaya—The power to take the form of anything or everything, to become visible or invisible.

Antaryamitva—The power to penetrate the heart and mind of others, to know all or to penetrate to the heart or center of anything and understand it totally.

There are many stories which illustrate the quality of Aeshvarya in Baba.

Once Baba said, "This week everyone will go without his or her favorite habit." There was one Margii however, who had a very strong attachment to chewing a particular type of tobacco and did not obey Baba's command. During the first day of that week, the Margii was walking with another Margii and chewing tobacco. Suddenly, to his amazement, the other Margii stopped still and gazed into space as if under some spell. Then that Margii turned to him and spoke in the same tone of voice as Baba, saying, "I told you not to do that."

The first Margii was even more amazed and shocked. He took the tobacco out at once and did not chew it anymore that week.

At the end of the week, Baba had put up a list of all the Margiis who did not comply with His order. At the bottom of the list was this Margii's name, only it had a line through it.

While I was in jail, I had a similar experience. I was feeling depressed because I was not getting any support for the anti-police corruption (verbal) campaign I had started. I decided to watch a not-so-sentient movie that was being shown that day. When I went in to watch it, I felt Baba was not happy with me watching this film (particularly as I was still an LFT at the time), but I did not care and reasoned to myself that I would not do it again.

After the film, and still feeling guilty, I went to interview prisoners about police verbals. The first prisoner I spoke to flew into a rage and started shouting abuse at me. While what he said was totally unjustified and wrong, the force which came with the abuse stunned me. Never before have I experienced such force.

When he had stopped abusing me, I went to my cell and lay down shaking. My nerves were shattered. Then I experienced Baba telling me that it was He who was abusing me, because I had watched that movie and thought that I could excuse myself by saying that I would not do it again.

When I recovered, I went to interview another prisoner, only to find the prisoner who had just abused me was accompanying him. Nervously I asked about police verballing, only to be surprised to find the abusive prisoner had suddenly become very friendly. He even offered to help with the interviews. *Baba Krpahi Kevalam.*

"The greater the height reached by a person, inspired by a great ideal, the lesser shall be his or her sense of pleasure and pain."

While I was an elected delegate of the Prisoners' Grievance Committee, by His Grace some positive achievements were made for the prisoners. The prison officers greatly resented this and so one night they arranged for me to be transferred without notice ("shanghaied") to one of the worst jails in the State. There I faced threats of violence from some prisoners as well as harassment and persecution from the prison officers. They tried to set me up on false charges so that I could be put in solitary confinement where they could abuse me.

While all this was going on, I was very worried. One night during sadhana, I heard strange voices and felt energy rushing through me. This went on for a few evenings. At first it only happened during sadhana, then it continued when I lay down to sleep. It got worse and I felt my mind was becoming lost in an abyss. I began to feel quite frightened and concerned. Suddenly, as clearly as if I had turned on a radio, Baba started talking to me. He began by saying, "I don't care if..." I could not hear or understand the rest of the sentence because I was more concerned with not losing my mind. But Baba kept on repeating: "I don't care if..." in a very serious and strong tone, meaning something like "Don't be afraid. I will look after you."

Finally, while Baba kept on with these words, I got into such a state of fright, frustration and surrender I just said to Baba, "All I want is Your love." Immediately the voices and energy rushes stopped and my mind returned to normal. A few days later I was transferred to the best jail in the State where my two co-accused were.

One time Baba was using His power of *antarayamitva* to see into the mind of a sadhaka doing sadhana. Baba lamented that many Margiis do not do sadhana properly and then scolded this particular sadhaka for thinking about so many worldly things.

Baba said that if our concentration is not good, then we should do more *shuddhis*. For example, if we have one hour for sadhana, three-quarters of an hour should be spent on the *shuddhis*, and fifteen minutes for *japa* or *dhyana*. If sadhana is still not good, then three-quarters of an hour should be used for kiirtan, ten minutes for shuddhis and the rest for japa or dhyana. Third and fifth lesson are also good for improving concentration. He also said that if there is no bliss in sadhana, then it means there is no devotion. Hence, we should do more kiirtan and think more of Him during the day.

A Margii told me of a story when he was at darshan and, while Baba was talking, he was thinking to himself, "I have such an uncontrollable temper, I do not deserve to be a Margii. I think I'll leave Ananda Marga." At that moment, Baba called the Margii up front to sit next to Him. While he was sitting next to Baba, the Margii was thinking how he would like to touch Baba, but would not do it unless Baba first touched him. Then Baba touched him behind the neck and immediately his bad temper disappeared forever.

Baba had been criticizing a Dada whose mind was on a project he had to do, instead of thinking about his mantra. Baba said that he should do a lot of kiirtan before doing sadhana. Dada replied that he did a lot of kiirtan but his concentration was still poor. Baba was quiet for awhile. Then he said, "Before starting sadhana you should take the same determination as Lord Buddha. Remember this:

Vishva yadi cale ya'y ka'ndite ka'ndite
Eka'a'mi vase nave samka'lpa sa'dhite

'Even if this Universe disappears crying, I will sit alone until I realize my Self.'"

"If people keep bad company, their psychic bodies will be misguided by the negative physical and psychic energies of those bad elements. Mental restlessness and the unhealthy waves of the environment will cause them to stray from the path. Hence, each and every human being should keep good company. One should move according to the spiritual flow and not according to the psychic flow of others."

Baba was walking with a group of devotees when he asked if they would do whatever he asked. They all said, "Yes." After walking along some more, they came across the rotting carcass of a dog which was full of maggots. Baba asked for a volunteer to eat some of the carcass. The devotees remained stunned for some time, until finally one person said that he would do what Baba had asked.

Approaching the dog's carcass, the devotee took his mantra and noticed a beautiful smell coming from it. As he took a bite, he experienced the nicest taste he had ever tasted. Explaining the devotee's experience to the others, Baba concluded that by using our Guru Mantra everything we experience can be transformed into something sweet.

"The problem with critics is that they don't create anything new and their minds become the object of their criticism."

A similar story occured when Baba was walking with a devotee and asked him what he saw when they came to some muddy water. The devotee said he saw muddy water. Baba told him to look closer. He then saw, by Baba's grace, divine light in the muddy water. After walking further they came across the rotting carcass of an animal. Baba again told him to look closer and when he did, he saw Divine light throughout the rotting carcass.

We cannot do sadhana all day, but we can practice our Guru and Ista mantras all day (the mantras of first and second lesson). By constant ideation we can reach the stage where all we perceive is Baba, divine light and bliss.

Once a Dada was at a dinner which he had been invited to attend by a top official. As per system, he took his guru mantra before eating. Sometime after the dinner, he met Baba. Baba told him that if he had not taken his guru mantra before eating, he would now be dead. The official was immoral and felt threatened by the ideals which Dada was teaching in the local town, so he had poisoned Dada's food.

After having done a lot of sadhana whilst in jail, and then being involved in jail politics, circumstances changed and my life became very unexciting. I was put in charge of cleaning the officers' toilets and the kitchen. Baba graced me with good ideation and so I found myself feeling that I was cleaning His toilet and kitchen. This made me very happy. Then I would go for a walk with my mantra repeating in my mind and the ideation that He was walking by my side. Anyone I met also became Him. This made me very contented and fulfilled. After that I lost a lot of interest in finding fulfillment and happiness in external work, realizing that it really is all within.

After coming out of jail and getting married, I applied this ideation to domestic chores and experienced the same bliss. I find that singing kiirtan is particularly helpful in creating this blissful ideation. And with my wife ideating and singing kiirtan as well, the whole atmosphere of our home becomes so happy and sweet. Our children seem to benefit from the positive atmosphere too.

> *"Spirituality is the base and fundament of life. Hence, all sorts of training should be 99.9% based on spirituality and 0.1% based on social, economic and political aspects. Nobody should be a fool to build a mansion on the bank of a river with quicksand."*

AESHVARYA • THE EIGHT OCCULT POWERS

force push her on to the road and in front of an oncoming truck. Immediately her mantra came to her mind, and she then felt an even stronger force push her back on to the safety of the footpath.

In jail I had a few experiences where repeating my mantra saved me from violent attack. On one occasion, a huge drunken prisoner wanted to fight me. Baba gave me the idea to ideate on Him. So I did and when I felt bliss, I projected it onto the aggressive prisoner. Suddenly he stopped abusing and threatening me and left. A few minutes passed and he returned, apologized to me and ended up becoming a friend.

Devotional ideation creates an integrated outlook which makes life positive, simple, carefree and blissful. Without spiritual ideation, our approach becomes analytical and life becomes negative, complex, worrisome and dry. Even worse however, is when the ideation suddenly disappears—life then becomes horrible. But Baba does that sometimes to remind us that it is by His sweet grace alone that we enjoy Him, and also to make us want Him even more and and to want worldly enjoyments even less.

> *"In this Vrndavana [the devotee's heart], both the devotee and the Lord are there. They are playing the game of hide and seek: now He attracts the devotee, now He hides Himself. When the devotee rushes to Him, he or she discovers that the One who was attracting from behind the scenes was close at hand, and so he or she attains Him. In this Vrndavana of the devotee's heart, Vrajagopala and Parthasarathi are mingled into One. Both are attracting devotees by bonds of love..."*

How few people can we fully trust—to whom we can tell all our pains and pleasures, to whom we can divulge all the thoughts of our minds and hearts and feel completely relieved, to whom we can say, 'O Lord, You know everything. I have nothing to hide from You.'   No, we do not ordinarily find such people. They are not only rare, they are also as sweet as honey. After coming into contact with such a person even once, one feels forever drawn to Him, one's heart yearns for Him, one cannot help but be pulled by His irresistible attraction. He is at the same time filled with sweetness and difficult to attain. One cannot get Him easily like puffed rice in the market place.   One cannot build a temple and permanently confine Him inside.   Even if one runs about the external world like a mad dog, one will not find Him. One will have to seek Him the most beloved, with the highest love in the innermost recesses of the heart, in the most solitary jewelcase of the mind."

On one occasion, after Baba had finished a talk about life, death and samsakaras, He did a practical demonstration. He told one of the Margiis to lie down and then he ordered the ten vital airs (*vayus*) to leave the Margii's body. Doctors were present and examined the body, proclaiming it clinically dead. The body was now icy cold due to all the vital airs being absent. Baba explained that his mind was now on another planet enjoying a lot of bliss and that he did not want to return. The Margiis began to worry because this dead margii had a family who would be shocked at hearing the news of his death. Baba then returned the vital airs to the dead man's body. After that the Margii explained that he had felt no pain when dying. Baba concluded by saying that we should have no fear of death as it is painless, rather like going to sleep and then 'waking up' in another body.

During one demonstration, Baba turned two Margiis into two giants, then two tigers, two skulls, two donkeys, two goats, two dogs, and then two lotus flowers. Next, a third Margii joined the other two to be changed into more animate and inanimate objects until they were changed into one copy of *Subhasita Samgraha* and finally, back into humans again. Baba concluded that everything is vibrational and if you can control vibrations, then not only can you change the shape of an object, but also its color, size, taste, etc.

Once in Ranchi, Baba called a boy to Him and asked, "With what do you see?"
The boy replied, "I see with my eyes."
"No, no, no. You see with your nose," Baba said.
So the boy began to see with his nose.
Baba said, "See with your tongue."
The power of vision came into the boy's tongue.
Then He said, "See with your ear," and the boy began to see with his ear. Baba explained, "Changing the power of the organs cannot be done even by siddhas. It is only by the power of Parama Purusa that this can be done. Parama Purusa can do anything He likes."

There were many disciples sitting with Baba on one occasion. Suddenly Baba called a boy and touched the boy's hand with His stick. He asked another brother to see what was in the stomach of that boy. That brother said, "Baba, it is cancer and it seems to be very dangerous."
Then Baba touched the boy again with His stick and said, "Look again. Has it been cured?"
The brother replied, "Yes, it seems to be ninety-percent cured."

Baba said, "Yes, I have cured it, but I have left ten percent. He will do sadhana and then it will be cured completely."

He touched the forehead (*ajina cakra*) of the boy who fell into samadhi. When the boy finally got up again, he felt drenched in bliss.

Baba said, "I have given this boy samadhi. Now you can see that there is a difference between an occultist and the sadguru. An occultist can cure disease, but no occultist can give samadhi to anybody. This can be done only by the power of the sadguru. Only the guru can give samadhi."

"To attain Him human beings should practice shravana *[constantly listening to elevating things],* manana *[constant spiritual thinking] and* nididya'sam *[constant meditation or fixing one's mind on the goal]. To attain Him one must penetrate deep within one's self, and for that the development of an introversial outlook is essential. An extroversial outlook will be of no assistance."*

Around 1963, Baba was sitting outside the Jamalpur ashram. All of a sudden, a cow entered the ashram. An avadhuta asked Baba, "Baba, does a cow have a kundalinii?"

"Yes," Baba replied. "Every creature that has a spine, has a kundalinii. Do you want to see the movement of the kundalinii of this cow?" They all said, "Yes". Then He made a movement with His hand and directed it towards the cow and the cow began to jump and dance. It seemed as if the cow was very happy. Baba said, "Just see, it is because of the rising of the kundalinii that she is feeling very happy and dancing. This cow will not live long. She will die, and after death she will become a human being."

Once three Margiis saw Baba in three different places on the same night. I know personally of two Margiis who have met Baba in Australia, even though at the time he was supposed to be locked up in jail in India. Since

His great departure, I know of Margiis who have still seen Him!

Baba has the power to project himself so that He can appear in different places at the same time. The only difference between Him and His forms is that His forms have no intestines and so cannot eat or drink and their voices are slightly different from His.

> *"This Great Director of the Great Drama has involved everyone in his or her own way. In doing so He finds happiness. He also does this to make things more interesting...In the drama He withdraws the bondage from a particular individual and liberates them. To place one in bondage and again release him or her is His liila."*

Besides referring to the eight occult powers, Aeshvarya also means an occult power or *siddhi*. Any sadhaka can develop these through the regular practice of sadhana. Even if one just sits down with eyes closed, she or he will develop some mental power within about six months. But getting an occult power does not necessarily mean that you are progressing on the spiritual path.

Once an Avadhuta asked Baba, "How do you know if you are making progress?" Baba replied that the two signs of spiritual progress are an increase in the radius of your love, and an increase in positivity. Occult powers are not signs that you are progressing—they are mundane.

The more you love people, the more you know you are progressing. And your radius of love will expand beyond people to animals, plants and even inanimate objects.

Since Baba is controlling our sadhana, any power that we may get is purely by His grace. Many of us have developed siddhis, but He does not allow us to feel them because there is a big chance they will be misused by our small egos.

Of the four stages of sadhana—*Yatamana* (struggle), *Vyatireka* (bliss), *Ekendriya* (occult power) and *Vashiikara* (self-control)—it is in the stage of Ekendriya where many occult powers are developed. This is considered the most dangerous and difficult stage to get through. Although the sadhaka has lost attraction for the mundane world, she or he now has to overcome the attraction of the supra-mundane world.

One reason for becoming a luminous body is the strong desire to obtain occult powers (*Kinnara*). Luminous bodies are sadhakas who in their last life were very advanced spiritually, but due to a very strong attachment to something other than God, they were born into a luminous body to exhaust their unusual samskara. It takes a very long time for the samskara to be completed and when it is, they are reborn again as humans and then get liberated. People often mistake these luminous bodies for ghosts or spirits (which do not exist at all) and feel frightened of them. We should not fear them though, as all they want to do is to serve us, to help exhaust their samskaras.

The other reasons for becoming a luminous body are: *Yaksa* — a strong attachment to money; *Kinnara* — a strong desire to become handsome or beautiful; *Vidyadhara* — a strong desire to gain name and fame; *Gandharva* — a strong attachment to music or the fine arts; *Prakrtiliina* — a strong attachment to the worship of Prakrti instead of Purusa; *Videhaliina* — awaiting rebirth into the next body after the death of the present one; and *Siddha* — a strong attachment to sadhana instead of Parama Purusa.

There are physical bondages, psychic bondages and spiritual bondages. All are bondages, no matter how great and wonderful they may seem and so no other desire than for the eternally free Parama Purusa should be cultivated.

Baba's powers are unlimited. He is omnipotent and omnipresent. Only Bhagavan is all-powerful and all-pervading. Others may become completely realized or become a Siddha (perfect), but they are not omnipotent or omnipresent.

The one who has Aeshvarya is called Iishvara, but Iishvara is not Bhagavan as He needs the other five qualities which I'll talk about in the next chapters.

AESHVARYA • THE EIGHT OCCULT POWERS

Bhagavan, You are the omnipotent and omnipresent One
   You have the power to become big or small,
      To control or know all
   Even the siddha has not the powers you possess
      But above all this,
The greatest power you have is to love all and hate none
This Divine Love of Yours is truly the greatest power of all.
                      —Narada Muni

2
Pratap:
The Balance of Love

The quality *Pratap* means to rule over and to love. The one who possesses Pratap will at one time seem very loving and affectionate, but at other times will show anger and scold us when we do wrong. If Baba was to show love all the time or if He was always scolding us, then we would either become spoiled and not learn how to discriminate, or we could not bear to be in the presence of someone who was always chastising us. That is why Baba said He loves us and at the same time punishes us for our bad actions. It is out of love and benevolence that Baba has this dual personality.

Once Baba told one Dada to set up seventeen schools within the next month. At the end of the month when Dada reported back to Baba, He asked him how many schools he had set up. Dada said he had established fourteen schools, but Baba became very angry and said, "You said you would set up seventeen! You can now do 600 *tik tiks* for punishment!"

After some time, and when the Dada could hardly do any more tik tiks (standing then squatting), Baba told him to sit in the corner and do sadhana. With much pain, the Dada put his legs into lotus posture and began to meditate. Each second seemed like hours as his legs throbbed with pain.

After a few minutes, Baba went over to him and touched him on the head and he fell into samadhi.

There were many Dadas and Didis attending an RDS. Each wholetimer had to go and report to Baba on the work they had been doing. Baba would often take the role of President of the organisation rather than all-loving Guru. He could become very strict and serious and was often seen shouting or scolding someone. The time had come for one particular Dada to report to Baba. All of a sudden he became very frightened of what Baba might say or do to him. Out of fear, he hid under a car. Other Dadas tried to persuade him to come out but he wouldn't move. He even tried to say that he was not the Dada being called!

Whatever Bhagavan Baba does, it is done in the greatest way. When He appears angry, even the bravest Tantrika gets frightened and when He shows love, even the greatest sinner feels overwhelmed with joy. No one can match Bhagavan's personality and He can take on whatever personality He desires.

In the past there have been some sadhakas who thought Baba had lost His powers so they left the organisation, thinking Him to be a fake. Sometimes He seems the most unimportant and unimpressive person while at other times He will reveal so much power, love, knowledge and greatness that it will leave the beholder gasping in wonder and amazement. Bhagavan is not concerned with an external show to impress people. Bhagavan does only that which is necessary for dharma or His liila.

"Both sadhana and success are within your easy reach. The result is already secured within me. I shall give it to you at the appropriate time. Do not bother about it.

"Whether you are a sinner or virtuous, those who come to God are all the same to Him. He makes no distinctions. All will be liberated.

"You are all my beloved sons and daughters. Sometimes I appear harsh to some, but that is for love. If I were indifferent, then there would be no need for scolding or punishment.

"I want to see you all laughing. It gives me great pleasure when I see you laughing.

"Leave all cares unto me — O be blessed ."

— Baba (1967)

    Baba was in the bathroom brushing His teeth when suddenly He called out to His Personal Assistant (PA) who was in the next room, "Dada, what kind of toothpaste is this?"

    PA replied that it was the usual kind.

    Baba asked, "Are you sure? It tastes very strange?"

    PA replied that he was sure. As he was walking into the bathroom, he exclaimed, "Baba! That's shaving cream you're using!" Putting on His glasses, Baba said, "So it is. In the future I must wear my glasses when I clean my teeth."

    The mind boggles as one tries to understand His game.

It is a rare privilege to be alive when He is on the planet. One great seer of the early part of the twentieth century said that he would gladly give his right arm to live in the second half of that century.

Once Baba commented upon how much His devotees have to go through and yet they will not even be around to enjoy the fruits of their work and sacrifice—it will be the next generation who will enjoy Sadvipra Samaja (society guided by spiritual moralists). "But you know," Baba added, "One thing they wont have to enjoy is me."

Although of course, through deep dhyana and dreams we can always enjoy Him!

"While drawing unit entities towards Himself, He adopts various blissful forms. Sometimes He deeply loves His devotees, sometimes He lightly scolds His devotees and then deeply loves them; sometimes He provokes interest and excites curiosity in their minds. He saturates the devotees' minds with different Rasas [Cosmic flow] and brings them nearer to Himself—that is, He attracts   through many Rasas."

One Margii sister was attending a Sectorial Conference. She was breast feeding her baby. Normally it is not expected that a nursing mother should fast as all her nourishment goes into her milk and thus the body would become deprived and fatigued. However, this particular sister did not want to be any different from the others and so she fasted on the fast day.

During kiirtan, this same sister was watching the way another sister was looking at Baba's photo and was thinking how devoted the other sister was. Thinking this she looked at Baba's photo and to her amazement and delight a big smile came upon Baba's face and a beam of light came to her out of His forehead, filling her up with bliss.

There was a Margii who was under increasing pressure to take bribes at his workplace. But he knew that if he did, the all-knowing Baba would be aware of what he had done and would scold him. Then he reasoned that even Baba must sleep, so if he took the bribe when Baba slept, then He wouldn't know about it.

After taking the bribe late at night, the Margii stood in front of a photo of Baba, smoking a cigarette and thinking how clever he was.

After some time he attended DMC. Just as Baba was getting up to leave after finishing His discourse, He suddenly sat down again. He told everyone that there was a man present who thought that he could out-smart Parama Purusa by taking a bribe late at night when he thought He would be asleep. This man became very uncomfortable as he realized that Baba was talking about him.

Baba asked the person concerned to stand up, but that everyone had to promise that they would not hold anything against him. All of the 20,000 people who were present agreed. The man did not want to stand up, but thought it would be worse if he did not, and was pointed out by Baba.

Baba said that after taking the bribe, the man had stood in front of a picture of Him smoking a cigarette and thinking how smart he was. Finally, with a feeling of great embarrassment, he got up and everyone immediately turned and looked at him disapprovingly. Baba immediately snapped at them, "You promised not to hold anything against him!" Everyone quickly turned back to look at Baba.

We cannot do anything secretly.

"Those sadhakas whose minds are crude and inert are not able to apprehend even an iota of His sweet essence. That is why at the time of happiness their illusion-dulled mental waves seek to remain in smug oblivion, disregarding Him and at the time of sorrow they unduly find fault with Him, failing to understand His merciful dispensation that exists behind that sorrow."

Once an avadhuta was learning to drive a jeep when he suddenly lost control of the wheel and hit a tree. The jeep turned over and crushed his chest. He was rushed to hospital, but the doctor said that he didn't have a chance of survival. Some Margiis told Baba and so He quickly went to the hospital where the Dada lay unconscious. Baba entered the room where the Dada lay and stood looking at him. Dada awoke immediately. Baba smiled at him and left. After only one month, Dada had completely recovered.

One Dada told of a period when Baba was beating and scolding him a lot during reporting, yet in the evenings when he would give Baba a massage, Baba would be extremely sweet. Dada didn't like the scoldings and beatings, but even more, he had a nagging feeling in his mind that Baba was a hypocrite—being cruel one moment and sweet the next.

Naturally, he didn't want to express these feelings to Baba, but one evening Baba asked insistently for Dada to express his thoughts. Finally Dada expressed his concerns. Baba said, "It's true that I give you very hard punishments and that I beat you. But isn't it better to receive punishment from me than from Prakriti (nature)? When Prakriti gives punishment she is ruthless. She is a blind force. The nature of fire is to burn. It doesn't care if it is burning iron or a baby's hand. So if you have made a mistake, your samskaras will be very bad and merciless Prakriti will give you punishment. So if I give you punishment, isn't that better than Prakrti?"

One time Baba was beating a Dada. Suddenly the Dada ran from the room and left his acharyaship and Ananda Marga as well. He said that he could not tolerate Baba's beatings any more.

Baba commented that had Dada endured the punishment a little longer he would have been cured of cancer. Now his future is not very bright!

Baba used to beat His workers to remove their negative samskaras and speed up their progress. But He also gives this purification to all Margiis indirectly by the clash He gives when we are doing sadhana and organisational work. Once Baba asked a Dada why a certain Wholetimer had just left Ananda Marga. Dada replied that this worker said he could not tolerate the persecution he was recieving from his higher authority (the Dada in-charge). Baba commented, "Doesn't Dada understand that nothing stays the same for ever? Everything is systaltic and changing. Had he stayed, eventually his situation would have improved."

Sometimes Baba may seem harsh and at other times very loving, but to His devotees He is always loving. Even when He beats His devotees, they say that they feel extremely fortunate and graced as they know that it is purifying them and making them realize Him more. Bhagavan Baba is Shiva, the benevolent one.

"A spiritual preceptor or Sadguru is necessary — His Grace is indispensable. His Grace is but God's Grace, for God is the ocean."

3
Yasha:
A Mixed Reputation

Yasha means "reputation". In the *Bhagavad Giita*, Bhagavan Shrii Krsna tells Arjuna, "To protect the righteous and to destory the wicked, to establish Dharma firmly, I take birth age after age." So it is said in philosophy that Taraka Brahma comes every 3500 years to liberate His devotees, destroy the *adharmik* forces and establish dharma. During this fight Bhagavan naturally gets both a good and a bad reputation. Among those who fight with Him and for dharma, He has a good reputation (*yasha*). Those who oppose him, hold him in ill repute (*ayasha*).

"Human civilization now faces the final moment of the critical juncture. The dawn of a glorious new era is on its one side and the worn-out skeleton of the past on the other. Humanity has to adopt either of these two.

You are the spiritual soldiers. You are the worshippers of life Divine. Hence, I call on you to adorn this crimson dawn deluged with glorious light.

Victory is surely yours."
—Baba's Vanii (1967)

When Bhagavan is alive, the world becomes polarized between the dharmik and adharmik forces. There is no neutral force, although in the beginning some will try to remain neutral. But as corruption, injustice and immorality reach their peak, it becomes impossible not to take sides. It is by this polarization alone that Bhagavan can be recognized. Baba said at this degenerative stage right becomes wrong, and wrong becomes right. Rational becomes irrational and visa versa. The rational and righteous are abused as irrational and unjust.

This polarization took place during the times of both Bhagavan Shrii Krsna and Bhagavan Sadashiva. During Shrii Krsna's time there were the adharmik Kauravas fighting against Krsna and the dharmik Pandavas. During the time of Sadashiva, there were the adharmik Aryans fighting against Sadashiva and the dharmik non-Aryans of India. In both cases the odds were in favour of the adharmik forces because of their size and strength. But because the dharmik forces had Bhagavan on their side, they ultimately won. Bhagavan's spiritual force is millions of times more powerful than the material force and so the spiritual moralists won in the end.

In Baba's early life, including the early days of Ananda Marga, He was the easily accessible and very sweet *Vraja Baba* of Jamalpur. But as His reputation began polarizing people, the stern *parthasarathi* aspect became more predominant. This has been the case particularly since the persecution of Ananda Marga and the direct persecution of Baba (in the beginning of the seventies). We then saw Baba mostly as the *Parthasarathi Baba* (of Calcutta), mobilizing and directing His organization into top gear for a war to re-establish dharma.

Today this planet faces the same predicament it faced during the time of both Shiva and Krsna. The immoral forces have all the power and because of the large numbers on their side, they seem to have the odds in their favour. But as they continue to mercilessly exploit others, they will shrink in number. Even then it may be too late for the pious sadhakas to overcome the adharmik exploiters alone. However, because of Bhagavan Shrii Shrii Anandamurtiji, all the righteous people will eventually come under His guidance. By His spiritual grace, they will defeat the evil forces.

India will emerge as a great power, but for that it will have to undergo a great struggle. Apparently, this will be a painful stage but there will be born a great Messiah in that country who will assemble thousands of little, little people and infuse in them so much courage and conviction that these very little people will collide against the powerful materialists and will disprove their claims and values. Afterwards, simpletons and the sincere will receive regard and respect. In the meantime, while the conditions of deceit, fraud, murder, theft and robbery will become very much rampant, human values will equally develop out of much clash and cohesion. But this emergence will not be stationary... after this, it will be the world of love, compassion, kindness, integrity, benevolence and brotherhood.

—Bovisha Silvigar, Hungarian Prophet

One should never doubt for a moment that Bhagavan Baba will establish Dharma as He has said. There are only two things which He cannot do-He cannot hate anyone and He cannot create another Parama Purusa. He can establish Dharma. The fact that Bhagavan came with His *samkalpa* (firm determination) to establish Dharma means that it will be done. He said that even if His disciples will not work for Him, He would establish Sadvipra Samaja (the rule of the moralists) with the help of goats.

The prophecy of the Hungarian woman, Bovisha Silvigar, is only one of many prophecies that a man coming from India would, with the help of His devotees and their organization, create Dharma on this earth. Probably the most well-known and respected prophesier is Nostradamus. Among many of his predictions which came true were prophesies about Hitler and Napoleon. Not only did he give the correct dates and their histories, but even their names. In his predictions he stated,

A world famous person will take birth in some religious minded country of the East. That person, through His little and insignificant followers, will create an upsurge in the whole world. That historical Cosmic man will bring about such a great struggle that it will engulf each and every household in mutual conflict....

Shrii Ananda Acharya mentioned in his prediction:

Dharma... will flourish in the form of an organized institution. Its founder and director will be a householder. He will prepare a systematic code right from the social obligations of man up to the pragmatism of world peace. People will doubt the utility in the age of materialism, but the oncoming catastrophes... will change the course of materialism. Then these very codes will be worshiped like the Vedas, the Bible... The keenness today for materialism will give way to the urge and anxiety for Atman.... Salvation. The state at the time of the Mahabrata will be taken up and this will be completed by this new religious organization.

A famous psychic, Anderson, said in his writings:

He will prepare one single constitution for all of mankind and one language, one world federation, one Supreme Court and one flag. He will instill in mankind a sense of compassion, [and His followers will be in newspaper headlines for their] exemplary service, sacrifice and courage.

Another respected psychic, Jule Burns, mentioned, among other things, how His devotees will fulfill their task:

His followers will manifest themselves in the form of a well established organization that in time will influence the whole world and will fulfill apparently impossible looking tasks early through devotion.

At a conferences of Yogiis, Astrologers and Saints in 1939, it was concluded that:

He [the Avatar] will be the controller of an organization and He will prepare detailed codes of human conduct right from the Supreme Being down to the principles of mutual conduct and these codes shall be acceptable to all logicians, rationalists and educated persons. He will be the great scientist of all scientists. [His greatest contribution will be] the investigation of Self and Atman.

A prediction found in 'The Astrologer's Handbook' is:

New forms of government and political concepts will be brought into being out of necessity. The end of this period will produce the beginning of world government. At that time [early 21st century], a new civilization will be born, based on enlightened humanitarianism and on a science using new technology and new forms of energy. This will mark the beginning of a thousand years of peace."

The Hopi people of North American have an ancient prediction called the "Hopi Prophecy". In it they say that great catastrophies will arise at the turn of the century, but the bringers of peace will bear the symbol of the svastika and the rising sun and wear "beehive hats".

And so they go on: A. Charles, Professor Harah, Professor Cheero, Jean Dixon and Mahatma Ram Chandra are a few more seers who point to Baba and His samkalpa. If you read the book, *Lord Has Come*, by Shrii R. N. Tyagi you will find another good example.

One Dada was from a Middle Eastern country. Before initiation in Ananda Marga he had been close to a Sufi master. After his initiation he decided to go to Calcutta to meet Baba. He arrived in Calcutta after several weeks of overland travel. He spoke neither English nor Bengali so he felt rather bewildered.

When he saw Baba for the first time coming out from His Lake Gardens residence Baba was in an angry mood and seemed like a madman shouting and scolding all the acharyas around Him. His rage seemed uncontrollable and He was stabbing the air around Him with His walking stick like a sword.

Dada thought, "How can my guru be this madman?" To add to his confusion and disappointment he saw acharyas also shouting and running about treating people with no consideration. So Dada became very disillusioned. Still he remained in Calcutta for a little while longer.

Once he happened to be standing right in front of Baba as He got out of the car. Baba looked into his eyes and gave His namaskar and a very sweet smile. Dada returned to his homeland after a few weeks.

Upon his return he went to visit the Sufi master who questioned him about his sudden disappearance. Not knowing what to say he pulled out a photo of Baba and said, "I went to visit this man. Can you say something about Him?"

The sufi master looked at Baba's photo for a while, and then said, "He is the real master. He can change any vibration in this universe just by willing it."

Dada protested, "He behaved like a madman and his disciples were even worse! How can he be the Master?"

The Sufi replied, "He is so great that He accepts everyone unconditionally. He has the power to transform anyone who will surrender to Him completely and make jewels out of them. He is hiding Himself so well that only those He chooses will be able to recognise Him. His influence will be felt in all aspects of life and there will be no subject left untouched by his teachings and writings. Volumes will be written in the future on His works. Society will recognise His greatness, long after His departure from the planet."

Dada asked, "If he hides himself, how can I know him?"

The Sufi replied, "There is no way." But after a few minutes he said, "Wait, there is one way. If one can understand divine love, one can know Him."

At that moment Dada decided to dedicate his life to Baba's service.

It has been said that Baba has branches of Ananda Marga on 52 planets. So you see His work of establishing Dharma is nothing new, nor has it been confined to this planet alone.

Once there was an American Margii who was walking in the mountains when he saw a flying saucer. As he was watching it he was wondering what he would like to say to it. Then he thought of just saying, "Baba Nam Kevalam" and so mentally he said that to the UFO. To his surprise and delight he got a message back from the UFO saying, "Oh no! He's not here as well is He?"

Once when Baba was in jail, he told the Dada staying with him that he didn't want to be disturbed. Just then a huge whitish figure appeared. All of a sudden, Baba went red with anger and He began to shout some strange language at the white figure. It vanished as suddenly as it had come.

After a while, Dada asked what had happened. Baba replied that it was a devotee from another planet. He was angry with the devotee for disturbing Him after He had just asked not to be disturbed.

> *"As democracy does not recognize any cardinal principles of morality, then rivalry, jealousy, meanness, immorality etc. take deep root and flourish unchecked. Moreover, the colour and form of democracy keeps changing because it continually gives importance to relative truths as its cardinal principles."*

Cast away all your doubts and fears, Bhagavan came here in the form of Mahapurusa, Shrii Shrii Anandamurtiji. Baba will protect you, help you, guide you and give you all the courage, strength and knowledge that you need to do His work. Victory has already been achieved by the fact of Bhagavan's advent. All that is needed is for it to manifest on the physical plane. The beauty of it all is that He has given us the task, thus giving us all the honour and glory.

Sometimes I have heard skeptical people, and even Margiis wonder how such simple Margiis can create a world government and establish Dharma. I remember once an acarya saying that when Sadvipra Samaja is established, humanity will look back at the Margiis and say that Baba must have been Taraka Brahma because His devotees could never have done it on their own.

A Didi asked, "Baba, we Margiis don't have so many skills and talents. But there are so many intellectuals and skillful people in the world. Why don't You utilize them to do your work?"

Baba replied, "What would be the greatness then?"

Once a devotee called Shankar Mukherjee told Baba, "You are always teaching us great ideas, but we have little talent. You should give those ideas to the leaders who can do something good."

Baba replied that the ideas which could be understood by him (the devotee) in five minutes would take two hours for leaders to understand. Only devotees can properly understand His teachings because they are all based on spirituality. The non-devotee or non-sadhaka always finds it difficult to understand matters concerning spirituality.

> *"When the devotee is able to hear, feel, realize and understand the will of Parama Purusa through having developed a relationship of love with Him, it is called a'pta va'kya. As devotees, you should follow only a'pta va'kya. You should remember that the Sixteen Points are your a'pta va'kya."*

As sure as Baba is Bhagavan, Dharma will be established. Once after Baba had finished talking about how Prout would be established in the world, one Margii repeatedly said that he could not see how it could be possible. With a great thundering voice Baba said that it was not impossible and that he would do it. Baba picked up the glass that He was drinking from and threw it against a rock, before walking away. The rock broke into little pieces and the glass remained unbroken.

> *"My love and my affection and my Blessings are always with You. But those who hold the flag continuously, marching to the tune of the Cosmic energy, they alone will be the heroes, and they alone will be able to carry on the task of the Supreme, and they alone will be the future vanguards, and they will create such a society that love and humanity will be established."*

Arjuna was on his way to pay his last respects to Shrii Krsna at the place where He had died. On the way there he was surrounded by thieves. Arjuna immediately drew out one of his arrows. When he tried to pull back the string of the mighty bow that Krsna had given him, he found that he no longer had the super-human strength that was needed. He realized that all the power and strength that he had was really given to him by Krsna. It was actually Krsna's strength that he possessed and now that Krsna was no longer physically alive, he had lost all that strength.

Ever since Baba came to this planet, He has been channelling special power and strength into His devotees so that they can do His work. But after He left, so that He will not have to return again like in the past, Baba is making His devotees collectively able to carry on with His work. Initially this will cause some clash, but after that will come much cohesion. Baba said that Parama Purusa utilises more and more of His *jiivas* (individual creations) to do His Work, rather than Him doing it directly. So through our ideation we can become mediums for Parama Purusa to work through.

Baba said that there are good sadhakas now but better ones will be born in the next generation, and the best will come from the following generation.

> *"In the fight against animality, hypocrisy and exploitation, victory is yours. You will establish PROUT, you will establish humanity. In the fight if your throat is cut, you will remain in my lap. During the fight against animality, if you die, you will get* Moksa *[final liberation] . If you remain alive, you will establish humanity.* Moksa *is in your hands."*

While on tour in Europe, Baba and His entourage suddenly had their visas for Italy cancelled. Baba remarked that the Italian authorities were afraid of Ananda Marga because, "We are better than the Hindus in philosophy. We are better than the Jains in asceticism. We are better than the Buddhists in morality. We are better than the Muslims in discipline. We are better than the Jews in orthodoxy. We are better than the Christians in social service. We are better than the communists in mobility."

(Baba also made indirect comments that the Catholic Church had been behind the visa cancellation. The Margiis observed that such a sudden legal action could only have come from someone in a very high place... such as the Pope himself.)

> *"Be ever ready to render service for the Marga. Never falter to or hesitate even to lay down your life for the ideals of the Marga. Remember, Salvation is assured on courting death with ideals of the Supreme. This is the reward of death in the battle of Dharma. This alone is the reward."*

Baba's mission produces the best qualities of all the other movements, plus its own uniqueness and greatness. To sum up Ananda Marga, it stands for the following seven points (as Baba said):
(1) Common spiritual ideology
(2) Strict moral code
(3) Socio-economic equality and security
(4) World fraternity
(5) Spiritual elevation in family life
(6) No caste, state, communal, national or geographical barriers
(7) No superstitions or dogma.

I have been told that Baba once said that when Sadvipra Samaja is established there will be 10,000 Jesus Christs and Vivekanandas (that is, Sadvipras), and that there will also be 3,000 acharyas.

Whether or not Baba actually did say this, only He really knows. It is an interesting thought though, and could well be true, knowing Baba. If it's true, then I can see some things that it implies.

Since Baba has said that there are no Sadvipras on this planet yet, it means that there is going to be much clash, growth and purification for the creation of Sadvipras. Much sacrifice, sadhana and service will have to occur. Yama and Niyama will have to be scrupulously followed. I put sacrifice first because really sadhana and service mean sacrifice. To sacrifice the ego at the altar of the Almighty is sadhana, and to sacrifice all your actions, all your personal desires and comforts to Him, to be His channel, is service.

> *"I will make Gods of my workers and great saints of my Margiis."*

Baba said, "People will recognize... Sadvipras by their conduct, devotion to service, dutifulness and moral integrity." And He said,

Human exploitation will not be tolerated. Rallying around the saffron flag, the symbol of sacrifice, they will devote themselves to the service of widely scattered units of the Human society and proclaim loudly, "Human beings of the world unite."

To be a sadvipra one must be established in Yama and Niyama and devoted to Cosmic Consciousness.

"Live for your Ideology, be one with your Ideology, fight for your Ideology, die for your Ideology."

The persecution that comes from His negative Yash (reputation) not only has social and historical lessons to teach humanity, but it also benefits His devotees. To be a devotee in Ananda Marga needs much surrender and a strong sense of selfless service. I have noticed those who leave Ananda Marga and Baba do so because they do not have sufficient faith, surrender or selfless service, three essential qualities for staying on the path of bliss.

The clash involved with being in Ananda Marga is certainly great and many elevated sadhakas have left because of it. Just before Baba's passing He mentioned that in the near future Ananda Marga will become so small we will need a "microscope" to see it. After some time it will then expand in size again.

The only Margiis that stay during this "microscopic" stage will be those whose only desire is to do service. They won't have any other personal motives like gaining name, fame, power or position. Nor will their motives be for more noble sentiments like justice, a desire for bliss or even to enjoy His physical presence. The only sentiment that must predominate in the Margiis hearts is to selflessly serve Baba through His organsiation. If our ego gets hurt or if we become frustrated or unhappy while serving His mission, then that is to be felt as His grace. The main thing is that we are pleasing Baba with our selfless service.

> *"Wherever organizational matters are concerned, I am physically there. Don't worry. You go and do your duty. I will be present."*

Baba once said that everyone should go to jail at least once in their life. While I would personally hate to go back to jail again, it was certainly very beneficial on a spiritual level. Any great hardship or sacrifice, if done with proper ideation, will greatly strengthen one's character and can lead to much spiritual elevation. That is why in the 16 points it states that we should always be ready to sacrifice ourselves for the ideology. In philosophy it is stated that if one is compelled to do something that is against one's nature then samskaras mature. There is the opportunity for great purification, provided of course that the action performed is a moral one.

For example, when a greedy person is compelled to be more generous or a shy person has to give a public talk, they can grow tremendously. Sometimes Baba breaks down weaknesses in our nature through this circumstantial pressure. While I was in jail I experienced some acute clash which made me want to run away. But in jail I couldn't run away and avoid the clash, so I had to confront it. While this was very painful, in time my mind became much stronger and the clash affected me much less.

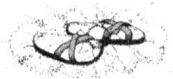

There are many examples of shy, unconfident persons going to acharya training and after some years as an acarya, being transformed into confident workers. Marrying and having children can also completely change one's nature because of the pressures and restrictions it places on our weaknesses. We can therefore see why Baba says we should choose one path or the other (by our late twenties if possible) because it regulates and directs our life in a purposeful way.

> *"A person with a dull brain cannot be a revolutionary. Hence one should be put in the most adverse and difficult circumstances and then left to come out of them by one's own effort. This will sharpen the brain and thinking capcity."*

Having a lifetime commitment also provides the opportunity for our deeper samskaras to be expressed. This will not happen if we think we can always leave if things get too difficult. Generally single life does not have any of the lifelong restraints, confrontations, or regulations of the *sannyasin* (renunciant) or householder paths. For most people the lack of such pressure would make the control of their lower instincts much more difficult. Baba says single people weaken the fabric of society, unless they have dedicated their life to some intense service work or cause.

> *"You should always think in terms of Ideology and collective interest and never in personal terms. Generally a stroke of difficulty or a blow to personal prestige or position diverts one's attention towards oneself, and the great Ideology is forgotten. This feeling may be either positive or negative but it preoccupies a large portion of the mind and thereby creates too much self-consciousness which makes one lazy and vocal. One then chats about oneself, one's difficulties, and one's relations with surrounding people. One loses balance of mind. In short, one then thinks all the time about oneself forgetting one's Ideology and task."*

Someone once commented that some Margiis were struggling to keep their marriages together. Baba said that they should, "Remain together—fight together. If we can't keep our small families together, how can we expect to become one world family?"

The only grounds for divorce in Ananda Marga are characterlessness, cruelty or irresponsibility. Otherwise, Baba says we should 'stick together.' He has also said to some newlyweds that they should practice "maximum tolerance" with each other. With their children, Baba says parents should give maximum love until they are five and give them what they want (within reason) —ie. there should be minimal restrictions. After five, He says that we should be very strict with our children, but that the strictness must be equal to our love. That is it should be firm, but with tact. After they reach the age of 16, we can soften the strictness and a relationship of friendship can develop. Baba said that to be successful parents, good judgment plus restraint are needed.

So we can see that all the clash that comes with either wholetimer or householder life is very beneficial to our growth. Struggle is the essence of life and whether we adopt the spiritual or worldly approach, clash will be there. So we may as well take the spiritual approach and get something worthwhile. Baba says that to give in to our weaknesses would be disastrous, Avidyamaya would "stab [us] as soon as our backs were turned." We must have strength and courage to walk the path of bliss. We must also possess a strong sense of selfless service.

> *"Vidya or Avidya — select any one of the two and the other is sure to stand aside... The avidya force declares war on those whose desire or inclination is towards vidya. This gives rise to a hostile tendency in the recesses of their minds, against which they have to struggle. At home, the husband, wife or the other members of the family become dissatisfied with them, and create various obstacles. In the field of their activities, the opportunities arise for depravity, meanness, taking bribes, etc. and they have to maintain their self-control. The locusts of desire come swarming in to destory the very bud of their sadhana. So they must carefully avoid such temptations for their own safety."*

Baba may appear harsh at times, but that is part of His benevolent nature. Baba once explained to some wholetimers that the reason He scolds them during reporting is to keep their attention focused upon Him (out of fear) and the reason he gives them impossible tasks to perform is to keep them thinking of Him. It creates pressure so they will keep thinking of Him. So they think "I must do more or Baba will scold me!" Be it through love or harshness, He brings us to Him.

> *"To ensure the subsistence of Acaryas, all kinds of sacrifice should be accepted."*

Once a Dada noticed Baba drawing something that looked like a flow chart. He asked what it was. Baba replied, "This is a sadvipra machine." Here are the phases one passes through to become a Sadvipra:

INITIATION
16 POINTS
ORGANIZATIONAL DUTY
WHOLETIMER or HOUSEHOLDER PATHS
PERSECUTION
SADVIPRA

At each of these stages a new and deeper commitment is made. At each commitment, and thereafter while trying to follow the commitment, clash and cohesion is experienced. This brings about progress. Many will leave the path, but those who do not will move on to the next stage. Those who pass through all the stages, due to their faith and surrender, will get adequately purified and elevated to become Sadvipras. Baba concluded that this was only one of His 'machines.'

This 'sadvipra machine' also shows how important Baba's organization is for our spiritual progress. I emphasize Baba's organization because Ananda Marga is His creation, His mission, His way of elevating us and serving creation. It cannot be separated from Him. Baba said that to know Him, we must do His mission.

> *"A family person is like a strong tree which is self-supporting while the Sannyasi is like the vine which twines around the tree for its support. A family person therefore deserves more respect than a sannyasi, according to... Ananda Marga."*

By getting involved with Ananda Marga, following the 16 points, taking on organizational duties, getting married or becoming a WT, and then going through the persecution that comes through association with His mission, we can attain sadviprahood. A sadvipra is an elevated sadhaka who is at one with Baba's flow or mission.

Baba said that He had worked out what was needed for this planet when He was just thirteen years old. All that was needed was the right time for its physical manifestation. That time is now. The bad reputation, persecution and struggle that comes with the manifestation of His mission should not be reason for despair, criticism or avoidance. Rather it is proof of His advent and ultimate success. We can only benefit by being an instrument in that manifestation.

What You are to me,
You may not be to others.
What You are to others,
You may not be to me
But what you are to Brahma
Oh my all-loving and beloved Guru,
I'll be that to You

—Narada Muni

4
Shrii:
Beauty, Charm & Energy

It is said that Shrii is a characteristic of that Divinity within us all. It is only because of maya's dominance in a person that Divinity cannot be perceived. When someone does the sadhana of the Great, then this Shrii in everything gradually becomes apparent in the sadhaka's mind and they too feel it within themselves. People are natually attracted to them.

Shrii can also be dangerous if one is egotistical. Some sadhakas use their charm and attraction to persuade others to do things for them which are not dharmik or according to the principles of Yama and Niyama. It is also true that one of the reasons for becoming a luminous body is because sadhana was done with the aim of becoming handsome or beautiful.

It is said in philosophy that to the ones who do not do Bhagavan's sadhana, He looks just like any ordinary man. They cannot see anything particularly great or attractive about Him. But those who do practice Bhagavan's sadhana, they alone get to realize some of His greatness, beauty and charm. I say some of His greatness because no one will every completely know His greatness—it is too vast and beyond "knowing."

His devotees get attracted to Him more and more. After a while devotees will feel peace and bliss—even Samadhi—just by looking at His photo, or hearing or singing His name, or just by thinking about Him. And as for being in His physical presence....what can one say? When all anxiety, fear, shame, sadness, hate, etc. are lost by thinking or singing about Him, words could not possibly describe what is like to be in Bhagavan's presence.

Before Baba's release from prison, many of Baba's devotees had never seen Him physically and yet they had sacrificed their whole life, all their personal desires and comforts, for Him without a single doubt or regret. Such is the universal Shrii of Bhagavan Baba. Just to see Baba in a dream can cause one to wake up with tears in their eyes, crying, "Baba, Baba" with tears of joy.

Even if one has not dreamt of Him, then there is no denying the wonderful feeling of closeness that one gets through doing His sadhana and service. It is no wonder that He is called Shrii Shrii Anandamurtiji (the embodiment of bliss). Even the greatest skeptic will fall in love with his personality if she or he does His sadhana and work.

One evening while Baba was on field walk, I was walking behind Him with several other guards. After some time, I noticed that each time Baba walked under a tree, it would come alive with the sound of birds singing. As soon as He passed from under the tree, the birds would stop singing, even though we guards were still walking under the tree.

During one darshan at Tiljala, I looked out the window and noticed all the fish in the pond below Baba were facing towards Him.

When Baba passes by in His car dogs stop fighting to watch Him, then return to fighting once He has passed. Once, as Baba passed a wedding, all the guests left the bride and groom to watch Baba drive past.

Baba's form is such a powerhouse of energy and bliss that no one can ignore His presence, even if it is just the sight of Him going by in the car. Humans, animals and plants are all affected and vibrated by His presence. The idea that His form is the point where Parama Purusa's love enters the universe seems apt.

> *"If someone really loves Him he or she is bound to say, 'Ah ! How nicely He speaks, how sweet is His language. How soft is His body, no one has ever experienced such softness. I have never seen such incomparable physical charm—how sweet is his smile... How blissful are all His expressions. It is difficult to say which expression is more charming.' That is why I say there is no second entity that is so beautiful, so pleasingly soft as our Vrajgopala."*

One very interesting phenomena in Ananda Marga is that all Margiis seem to have a similar appearance—their eyes all look the same. The eyes reflect one's state of mind and since all these multilateral Margii minds are doing the same sadhana of the Great (Baba's sadhana), it means that all these different minds are being gradually converted into the same Cosmic mind. That is also why there is a very strong feeling of brother/sister-hood in Ananda Marga. It is this same Cosmic sentiment that will create a world fraternity in the future. No human made barriers or distinctions, such as race, nationality, age, sex or profession, can keep the sadhakas separate. These false distinctions have no importance in Ananda Marga as far as spirituality is concerned. All are looked upon as manifestations of the Supreme Father and all are His children.

Sometimes Baba's attractiveness causes His devotees to become attached to Him physically and they forget about their duty and work. There was once a Didi who was spending more time visiting Baba than doing her work.

When Baba heard that she was there to see Him yet again, He said "What, is she here again? Hasn't she got any work to do ?!" She understood His message and left.

> *"...when you advance in the cult of sweet devotion, you enjoy more and more sweetness. While advancing, you enjoy bliss at every step. Obviously, at that stage, you don't like the tormenting harshness of knowledge and action."*

While Baba's form is extremely attractive, and also has great spiritual significance, we must not forget that Baba is not really the body but Supreme Consciousness situated in our *Sahasrara cakra*. To experience the inner Baba is to experience the real Baba.

By His grace, we can experience Him internally in many different ways—in sadhana, in dreams and in daily ideation. Actually, the inner experiences are greater because they are not limited by the restrictions of the external world—by time, place and person. Baba can spend as much time as He wants with us internally—and in any way He wants. He can be so sweet and intimate. While He can be very sweet and intimate externally, it is a fact of spiritual life that the inner world of the devotee is sweeter.

> "...the inner expression of Parama Purusa in the human ectoplasmic world [the mind] is decidedly more sublime than His manifestation in the outer world. For He is drawing human beings, attracting them in their ectoplasmic world. He says, "Come along, come to me. You will have to come." Humanity cannot but respond to His irresistible call."

Once Baba explained that love is internal and psychic, not physical. Being physically close to someone, including Guru, does not necessarily produce love. Only by constant ideation on the beloved can true love arise. Baba said if physical closeness was all that was needed for spiritual elevation, then His shoes should be liberated!

Once a former Personal Assistant (PA) of Baba, Dada Ramananda, said that at times, he felt closer to Baba when he was doing relief work than he did when he was Baba's PA. The fact that Baba's PA and others physically close to Him still have to do sadhana regularly proves that physical contract is not the goal. Of course, being in His physical presence can make it easier to ideate on Him, but this is not necessarily so—and there is the danger of too much contact making one dependent on His physical presence for inspiration.

Baba has always discouraged a personality cult, saying that He wants people to come to Ananda Marga because of its ideology and not because of Him. Although to begin with some may be attracted by Baba, gradually they have to get attraction for His ideology. That is what will last since He has left his body.

If devotees get too attached to His form, then when He leaves physically, they will have difficulty staying on the path, having nothing to inspire them. And this is what happened to many after His *Mahaprayan* (physical death).

With hindsight, we could see that more and more Baba was weaning His devotees from His physical presence before He left.This was so that they had to turn more to the internal Baba for guidance and inspiration. Also by making His devotees less dependent upon His physical form, He was preparing them for the future when He was no longer present. But more than this, He was teaching His devotees to enjoy Him internally in His many forms of ectoplasmic bliss.

One cannot remain away from Him. Rather one has to rush alone towards Him, because there is that inseparable bond, the inferential bondage of the Cosmic flow.

Baba writes so beautifully in the book *Namah Shivaya Shantaya* of one of these forms of ectoplasmic bliss—the world of dreams:

The person's life is successful who dreams about Parama Purusa.

"I saw Him in a dream. In a dream I made His acquaintance. In a dream I loved Him. In a dream I called to Him, 'O Lord, full of love.'"

In the lives of many people, a time may come when their days are full of the thorns of miseries but at night, during dream, they transcend their pains and pleasures. Then, meeting their Ista in dream, they beam with joy and laughter in the ocean of bliss ... those who experience this kind of dream are truly fortunate. It is they who say, "I do not see Him with my eyes. I see Him in my mind. In that beautiful meeting, all sorrows disappear. In dream I am alive—in waking, I forget."

Even in the waking state, their lives are drenched in the drowsy sweetness of that dreamy atmosphere, and then in their lives, that dream becomes a reality. As a result, the waking state for them becomes meaningless.

Then cannot those dreamy persons do any good to the society? Yes, certainly they can, and in a better way. This state of drowsiness is not dullness or crudeness; rather it is the golden opportunity to fully utilize one's existence by touching the feet of Taraka Brahama.

Dada Santosananda gives a beautiful account of enjoying Baba in dreams (and other ectoplasmic ways):

> When I retire to sleep, you keep my head in Your lap. What a grace divine! You lovingly continue to give me your factual company. And I move with you, by Your grace, Baba. In the fantastic world of heart warming dreams, You take me from one planet to another, from one star to another, from one stratum of experience to another. From this colourful world of dreams when I slip into the state of sleep, in that state of thoughtlessness, You continue to stay with me as a loving companion.
>
> When I return from that state of mental calmness, from the state of virtual unconsciousness, to the state of sub-consciousness, I find and feel You in indescribable handsome appearance. You play with me and You dance with me. You express Your love variously. You love me with overwhelming intimacy and kindly let me feel "I am Your nearest and dearest." You show me the beauty and sanctity of Your love. And through these exciting experiences you bring me back, slowly and sweetly, to wakeful state.

After my conviction, I decided that the only way I would be able to cope with my time in prison was to do maximum sadhana. This I did for some time until I felt Baba telling me to do more worldly service. During the times of long sadhana, Baba would often appear in my mind. He was so clear sometimes that I thought my eyes were open. He was so vibrant, shining and inspiring—and would often appear in Varabhaya mudra. One time He mocked me by appearing and then leaning over to one side. I suddenly understood that Baba was telling me that I was leaning over in my sadhana. Baba vanished and I quickly straightened up.

> *"When the devotee is with Him in the presence of others, they feel that it would have been nicer if I could have enjoyed His company alone [and] enjoyed His company more intimately, more closely. I am not pleased that He is with others... I feel happier when I think that He is mine only. When we are alone, it seems He is only mine, and I forget what I should say to Him ..."*

One great devotee, Dada Dasarathaji, narrated this story many years ago:

> I had been doing sadhana for some four or five years. It is my practice to do sastaunga pranam [prostration, lying face down] in the very beginning of sadhana. That day, too, I did the same. But I remained slightly longer than usual in that posture—I do not know exactly how long—it could have been a couple of minutes, may be even three or four minutes or even more than that. I had possibly fallen asleep. Suddenly I clearly heard within me Baba's voice calling, "Master Sahab [Sir], Master Sahab. Master Sahab!" The voice was from within me and Baba addressed me by this name jocularly and so sweetly. The second address was sweeter than the first, and the third was the sweetest. I regained my consciousness, got up from Sastaunga posture and started my sadhana in the proper asana [position]. Had He not taken the trouble to wake me up, I might have wasted the fine morning in only sleeping.

Another rare ability, unique to Taraka Brahma Anandamurti, is to give others the experience of the Universal Form of Parama Purusa. This was once given to Arjuna on the battlefield by Lord Krsna. Dada Parameshvarananda recounts the blissful experience of Baba's Universal Form which Baba graciously allowed him to experience:

> ...Lord called my name, and as per His wish, I at once came very close to Him, where He was sitting on the cot in a gracious form. Then He told me to be seated in bound lotus posture keeping my spinal chord straight. He touched my eyebrow centre (*Ajina cakra*) with His finger and ordered me to concentrate my mind in the pineal gland centre (*Sahashrara cakra*).

With His touch, my whole body and mind became purified and started vibrating with spiritual current. After a while, the Lord ordered me to penetrate my mind and to see each and every part of my body. The moment He ordered this, I started seeing Sadguru Anandamurti present in each and every molecule of my flesh in the affectionate and gracious posture of Varabhaya mudra, with smiling and charming face. He was not there in a body made of flesh, blood, bones, etc, but in the Divine form of effulgence. Then He ordered me to withdraw my mind from the flesh and to enter into and visualize each and every part of the bones of my body. I did accordingly and saw the same glittering, shining and fascinating Divine form made of effulgence.

Afterwards, He ordered my mind to expand and see into all the solid factors of the universe. I visualized that vast solid factor with millions of planets, galaxies, nebulae and stars, as all the things were in my mind. It was really unique, strange, miraculous, unbelievable and unimaginable. Lord Anandamurti was sitting everywhere in the gracious and effulgent form of Varabhaya posture with His ever-smiling face. Thereafter He ordered my mind to cross, penetrate, expand and see the liquid, luminous, aerial and etherial factors respectively. My mind was visualizing His Divine form accordingly without any effort, merely by His grace and wish.

At last He commanded my mind to expand into each and every atom and particle of this universe. They were innumerable and countless. Lord Anandamurti was sitting in each and every particle in the posture of Varabhaya mudra with smiling face. His form was made of Divine effulgence and was more bright and shining than the light of millions and millions of suns.

By visualizing and realizing this universal form of Sadguru Baba, my mind entered into the formless state. Thus my unit consciousness was completely merged into the Divine ocean of Supreme Consciousness and I forgot about my surroundings. After that, I did not know when the Lord and devotees left the room.

When I regained my consciousness and came back to the normal mood, that Divine impression was still in my mind, and I enjoyed that state for many months. When I remember those Divine experiences, I still feel much spiritual inspiration and enlightenment and it gives me new light, vision and energy in my body, mind and soul.

> *"The more the Sadhaka advances, the more his or her qualities change...one loses one's former qualities and assumes the qualities of the object of ideation."*

The outstanding and attractive qualities of Baba are shown as He narrates the experience of His own birth and childhood:

I am in my mother's womb. From there itself, I can see my mother and I recognize her so well. I see my father, my sister and my other relations. How well I know them! And I know their names, too!

I am born. Normally children weep at birth. I don't—I am all smiles. I am happy to be born. I want to address the people around me by their names because I know them so very well. But alas, how incapacitated I am! My vocal chord does not permit my voice to come out.

They want to feed me. They have put a piece of cotton in a cup containing milk. Drop by drop the cotton will drop milk in my mouth. How silly of these people! Am I a child to be fed in this manner? I shall drink with the cup, not the cotton. In protest I raise my hand and hold the cup. They are taken aback at what I have done. I realize that I have done much to perplex them and I return to being a child just born.

I grow up. To move about I have to crawl. How painful it is! My elbows and knees are full of aches. How long is this going to last? I notice someone speaking into my ears, "Just a few days more."

I don't see him. Who is he? But his voice is around me whenever I am dejected. What a consolation he showers on me by telling me that this painful affair won't be much longer!

I grow up a little more. I am sleeping by my mother's side. In the dead of night I am awakened. What I see is so unusual! My entire being, my mother's being, the cot, the room, the space beyond, is all full of such a sweet effulgence! I enjoy seeing it. I am lost more and more in it. I wonder what would happen to my mother had she, too, seen this all-engulfing light.

Baba went on to explain more about His childhood experiences with this strange voice talking to him. Finally He asked Dada Amitananda what it all meant? Dada did not know and while Baba was away he asked another Dada who replied: "It was a part of Baba's being which was projecting and talking to Him, helping Him and guiding Him. It is part of His unconscious."

Baba came back and asked again if Dada knew the answer. He said he did not, but repeated what the other Dada had said. Dada Amitananda asked if this was correct and Baba smiled and said,

Naham manye suvedeti no na vedeti veda ca,
Ya nastadveda tadveda no na vedeti veda cat

"Neither do I say that I know Him, nor do I say I don't know Him, because I know that He is beyond my 'knowing' and 'not knowing.'"

It was during Baba's childhood, at the age of five, that one day He came across a column of light. Baba asked, "Who are you?" The reply came that it was Anandamurti. That light then merged into Baba—and He became "Anandamurti," the embodiment of bliss.

Something which even a thousand births could not give, Baba can give in a few seconds. Even Nirvakalpa Samadhi, the highest samadhi or stage of consciousness that one can reach, Baba has given to many of His devotees. I heard of a Dada who, for a time, experienced Nirvikalpa Samadhi every time he attended one of Baba's darshans.

Baba's quality of Shrii, as well as His qualities of Aeshvarya and Pratap, are shown in this story told by a devotee.

Baba said to me, "My boy, you are having impure thoughts." I told Him "no," but He held me by the ears and told me that I had had them recently. I remembered them and admitted the fact to Him and He told me of other days when I had had the same impure thoughts.

Then He told me that I was a good boy, that I was not really bad and that I should call Him Baba. He made me draw near to Him and put my hands on my chest in the gesture of namaskar. I placed the two thumbs of my hands below my breast and He told me to bring them higher. I did so, but it was not high enough. He placed His finger on the spot and as I fixed my gaze on that spot, it seemed that I lost all track of time. When I returned to consciousness, my hands were still on that spot and I was still gazing at that spot, but I knew some moments had already passed.

He then told me to stand up and to gaze into His eyes. As I did so, I seemed to see balls of fire in His eyes and I could not look at them for very long. I embraced Him as He had told me to do and, at that moment, it seemed as if His body entered into mine and mine into His. We became merged into one inseparable body. I felt thrilled and I think I huddled to Him with closer feeling, energy and confidence pouring into my whole system.

As we separated, He touched my left rib and told me that I was not in perfect health. He said I should avoid drinking wine with a high percentage of alcohol and that I should cut down my smoking to a minimum. I told Him of a certain ailment that I had and he said that He has given me the hint for its cure. I suppose He has.

"Are you a good boy?" He asked. I said that I am now, but before I was not so good. He got angry and said that I have always been a good boy and that I should never again think that I have been bad because he is already with me. I nodded my head in reverent agreement.

This is just one story typical of those told by many who have been vibrated by Baba's physical presence. Baba's face seems to glow—so soft and pure and without any sign of aging. His eyes seem fathomless, eternal and infinite. In fact, His eyes are the Cosmic eyes—the Purusottama. He is so perfect, everything Baba does, is done perfectly. Even such a simple thing as walking seems to be done in the most perfect way by Baba. And when Baba smiles, from my own humble experience in person and in dreams, it is like the sun coming out after days and days of rain—such warmth and love that only Bhagavan Baba can give.

I remember the first time I saw Baba. It was at darshan at Lake Gardens. When I saw Him, it was as though my senses went numb. I could perceive that He was something great, something super-human, indeed Divine, with a definite glow about him and when He entered the room, the whole atmosphere electrified and uplifted. But I felt no feeling for him. It was not until after He had left, when my senses could regain their normal composure, that love, bliss and tears flooded through me.

Sometimes when the time comes to leave His physical presence, tears come at the thought of separation from Him—and not just at the thought of physical separation, but also the internal separation. When I am close to Him physically, I usually have time to do maximum sadhana and get close to Him internally—for there are no worldly duties to occupy my time or mind.

On one of my visits, as I was doing my last sadhana before leaving Him, He appeared in my sadhana and gave a deep, long parting namaskar. He seemed so sad that I was leaving. It made me feel so close and exclusively His. In the external world He is for everybody, but internally He can become mine and mine alone.

His appearance reminded me of the time while I was in jail when He used to come often in sadhana. One time I was feeling very clashed from jail politics when I sat down to do sadhana. Suddenly, He appeared beaming with the sweetest smile. His eyes were lit up with such love and penetration, He seemed to look right into my mind. Such a Divine sight, such beauty and charm. Such Shrii! Just the sight of him makes the day great. I love Him.

> *"The spirit of service comes from the spirit of serving the Supramental Entity. Where the spirit of serving the Supramental Entity is lacking there cannot be any service spirit. So pro-spiritual psychology is essential for a happy and integrated social order."*

Dada Samanvayananda writes an inspiring description of Baba and His charming qualities:

By His personal behaviour He would not allow anybody to know that He is Lord, that He is Bhagavan. He would talk with you, meet with you, like the most affectionate Father....

Sometimes when He is in the mood of preceptor, sometimes when He is in the mood of the Lord, then he would express something by which people could see and understand that He is Almighty, All-knowing and All-pervading.

Yes, He has control over rain, clouds, air, sun, moon, planets and stars. He can send your mental body to any planet and you can study there and then return. Loving Father allows you to know such higher things.

His simple touch, or a simple glimpse of him for seconds, inspires hundreds of poets, writers, orators, leaders, and singers. There are hundreds alive who have become these things by His touch and His darshan (Holy presence). Many ordinary persons now, by His grace, possess extraordinary mental faculties, occult powers and spiritually higher states called *siddhis*. This is the gift, the Divine gift of Baba, Supreme Father, to His children.

Sitting alone on a hilltop with him
I cast my eyes' vision out onto the material world
With wonder and delight I absorb some of the Lord's creation
Dark blue mountains stand tall with lush green valleys at their feet,
The spring's trees and flowers are blossoming and blooming
        with all their multi-colours.
As His name continues to flow with my breath,
I become amazed at how everything seems so much brighter today
I now feel much beauty and peace within my soul
As I turn my mind inward to dwell on the cause of all this
A strong conviction comes to me:
"Yes Lord, Your creation is truly beautiful.
But in comparison to You, all is black and white."

—Narada Muni

The late and great Dada Asiimananda describes a very beautiful experience which he had in March, 1969. He was with several others, enjoying Baba's darshan.

    Baba was rather unusual that day. Was He really unusual or did He only appear unusual to me? I am now unaware of the reality. But He was unusual, this is sure. He looked affectionately and penetratingly at each one of us and said in a very unusual voice (the voice appeared to me to be coming from some very remote place):
    "Soon there will be very difficult times. The great wind will remove from the trees all the old and withering leaves. Only the strong shall survive."
    I could not make out what He was hinting at—everything then was going on so smoothly.
    And then Baba asked us to do sadhana. The moment I closed my eyes I found my mind lose itself in vibrations of bliss. I was getting deeper and still deeper in a bottomless sea and the experience was so pleasant. I was feeling cut off gradually from the external physicality and was going deeper and deeper. I never wanted to return. My

mind was beholding sweet effulgence all over and I was engrossed in enjoying its sweetness. The mind-bee had stopped hovering and murmuring and was busy in drinking the endless nectar. I do not at all remember how long I was in this state.

Then I heard Baba's voice asking us to open our eyes. Unwillingly I obeyed. In between Baba's command to open my eyes and my sitting for sadhana, I had opened my eyes once and had found an all-pervading white effulgence engulfing everything. There was no object there, even Baba was not visible. I had again closed my eyes and continued my sadhana.

On Baba's command, when I opened my eyes again, I saw Baba in the Varabhaya Mudra. Baba was a different Baba, a very unusual Baba. I had beheld Baba earlier in the Varabhaya but never so majestic and great. Baba remained in the Varabhaya for such a long time—it must have been nothing less than five minutes. Not only were we lost in the fathomless ocean of the most absorbing beauty, Baba too was lost. Infinite time appeared to pass. Time had forgotten to click.

Finally Baba broke the spell, "Don't be afraid. You have no reason to be afraid." He was still in the Varabhaya.

And the wind that was to sweep the old and withering leaves started its fury in October 1971, two and a half years after this incident. The wind became a tornado in December, 1971. It is continuing unabated but truly, I have no reason to be afraid —I am under the shelter of His Varabhaya palm.

December 1971 was the start of a direct attack on Baba by the Indian government. He was imprisoned and later poisoned, and Ananda Marga was eventually banned during the 'State of Emergancy' of 1975. Baba was cleared of his murder charges in 1979 and the ban on Ananda Marga was lifted after the emergency ended.

Once Dada Dasarathajii was massaging Baba when he happened to notice some light coming out of Baba's feet.

"What is that light?" he asked.

"That light is a quarter of the effulgence of the Universe," Baba replied.

Shrii also means activity and energy. 'Sh' is the acoustic root of *rajaguna*, the mutative principle or active force. 'Ra' is the acoustic root of *bala* or energy. Together (i.e. Sh+Ra=Shrii) they mean the one who has much energy and utilizes it by doing much work (activity).

Unless physically or psychologically handicapped, everyone has energy and the capacity to use it. Many people unfortunately, are lazy and do not use much of their energy. Even some devotees will sing and pray to the Lord for strength when they already have it but do not utilize it properly.

If one has used up all their strength, then immediately Baba will give more. There is still no need to ask. All that is needed is for the sadhaka to start the work and Baba will provide what is needed to complete it (whatever He thinks 'completed' means).

"I have already given you the strength to do the work."

There was a doctor devotee of Madras who was given the duty of Prout. But he felt that he was not so experienced, and that he did not know enough and wasn't efficient enough. He wondered whether he was able to carry out this responsibility. This tussle was going on in his mind So he went to see Baba in Jamalpur planning to ask Baba to change has posting and to give it to some other responsible man. But out of fear of Baba, he didn't end up saying any of these things, though he thought about them.

Baba came to the Jamalpur ashram for darshan. He called forward an Avadhuta and made him sit on His lap. He said that if Parama Purusa so desires, He can give the power to see into anyone's mind.

"Divyananda, just see the mind of these people," Baba said. Divyananda began to see the minds of the people gathered.

Then Baba said, "If Parama Purusa so desires, He can give him the power to read thoughts." And he said, "Divyananda read the thoughts in their minds." Divyananda began to do it.

Then Baba said, "If Parama Purusa so desires He can give the power to read the thoughts of a man who is in America. Divyananda just see the man in America, and go into his mind and read his thoughts." Divyananda began to do it.

Baba said, "People think that they will do things, but it is Parama Purusa who does the things. If responsibility is given, the power is also given, and naturally if Parama Purusa wants, then men are made efficient. People should surrender to Parama Purusa and Parama Purusa will do the things."

Then Baba looked at that devotee and asked, "Do you understand?" The doctor laughed and kept silent. Then he went to Madras and began to work nicely.

"Whatever you speak or do, forget Him never. Keeping His name in your heart, work, remembering it is for Him. And, endlessly active, drift in bliss."

There are some who, relative to others, do not have much energy but still they keep active. They keep on working until the day they die. This is good. Better still, according to Baba, are those who keep working even while they are dying.

I should point out that being active or energetic is not the last word. There are many corrupt and immoral people who through their hard work have caused much poverty and exploitation. Knowledge without action is futile, but action without proper knowledge is destructive. At least the former will affect only the individual concerned, but the latter can also affect many others. All action, to be worthwhile, should be done with the ideation of pleasing the Supreme.

If while working we ideate that Baba is doing everything and we are merely His tools, then we won't 'burn-out.' I have noticed that before burn-out occurs, the sadhaka neglects his or her spiritual practices, especially kiirtan and *brahmacarya* (seeing God in everything), and becomes dry, cynical, critical and vain, loosing balance or *prama*. Even if burn-out doesn't occur, degeneration does, with eventual rejection of the spiritual path.

On the other hand, if we concentrate only on our spiritual practices and neglect our worldly relationships and duties, there will also be a loss in prama and we will feel a reaction. We can do sadhana all day and attain *savikalpa* and *nirvikalpa samadhis*, but Baba says our samskaras will still remain and can bring about our degeneration. In philosophy, one type of samskara is formed from our responsibilities (*kartavyagata*). If we neglect our worldly responsibilities to only do sadhana, later in this life or the next, this samskara will drag us back to fulfil this obligation— with interest. Therefore, for true progress, a balance between sadhana and service is needed. The main thing is to have proper ideation, otherwise our actions will generate a negative reaction.

We must not neglect our worldly responsibilities, but this does not mean we allow them to become the centre of our life either. Do what must be done, then leave it. We should not carry it with us or become obsessed with it. Baba must always be the centre of our life so that once our work is done and there is extra time, we should utilize it by doing more spiritual practices. Time is short and should not be wasted. This I understand to be the ideal to strive for.

> *"Yours is subjective approach through objective adjustment. But, while moving towards the Supreme Entity, you must do all your duties in the social, economic and other spheres. That is, your hands should be engaged in worldly duties, and your mind should be moving towards the Supreme Entity."*

Mahashrii Baba has created such a large and dynamic movement that in a very short time it has grown in almost every country of the world. In India, before the ban during the emergency, it had about two million followers and they were mostly from the intellectual class. In 1967, the *Current* newspaper in India commented:

> Ananda Marga has, during its short history, created a base in almost all the States [of India]. This was done at a striking pace and with great vigour....

All of this was done by Baba through His devotees' works. ERAWS (Education, Relief and Welfare Section), AMURT (Ananda Marga Universal Relief Team), RAWA (Renaissance Artists and Writers Association), RU (Renaissance Universal), WWD (Women's Welfare Department) and the other departments and trades of Ananda Margaa were created directly by Him.

Baba's socio-economic theory, PROUT, is a universal panacea to global problems. No other teacher has ever given such a comprehensive and practical blueprint for social welfare and progress.

Since Baba's release from prison, He created even more organizations and concepts. For example, the concepts of Neo Humanism, microvita, prama and the thousands of beautiful and multi-cultural songs of Prabhat Samgiita have enriched the cultural and philosophical base of Ananda Marga.

"While moving towards Him, do not neglect the world or the path of action. Although devotion is the most essential aid to help one to attain the Supreme Stance, yet knowledge and action are very important. Without them the possibility of downfall cannot be ruled out. Still for the sadhaka, devotion is the highest quality."

Once a small boy complained to Baba about his big duties. Baba laughed and said, "I give duties to everybody, even to babies. Their duty is to sleep, eat and cry."

Once when Baba was being carried into the prison, a top official of the Indian Central Bureau of Intelligence (CBI) suggested to Baba that since His wife and many Avadhutas had left Him and Ananda Marga seemed to be all but finished He should give up the idea of establishing PROUT. The CBI man said that if He did this they would arrange a comfortable lifestyle for Him.

Baba quickly replied, "Mind your business. You cannot keep me behind bars for long. Let Marga finish, let Marga go. I will re-establish not one but sixteen similar organizations." And He did.

Some of Baba's devotees were once visiting Baba in jail. He was greatly weakened by fasting and they began to help Him walk around His cell to give Him some exercise. As this was happening, Baba said, "You know, if I really wanted to, I could run around this cell." Then to the Margiis' surprise, He did.

While Baba was in jail and fasting, He always appeared, to the jail authorities to be very weak. But even after four years of fasting, when the authorities were not looking, He would maintain His strict routine of bath, shaving, asanas, sadhana, etc.

Baba is both charming and beautiful, active and energetic. He is also these qualities merged into one, that is, His activities are beautiful and his energies radiate charm. Whatever way you look at it, Baba is Shrii, the divinely attractive and dynamic One.

"If one thinks of obstacles, the obstacles themselves become one's goal, and the actual goal is relegated to the background. Hence in the sphere of Brahma sadhana only Brahma is the goal; only Brahma is to be meditated upon....To establish a heavenly kingdom in this mundane world human beings will have to fight tirelessly against the internal and external demons. But this does not mean that the demons should become the object of ideation."

5
Jinana:
Knowledge

Knowledge or *jinana* is of two types: one is worldly knowledge and the other is spiritual knowledge. Worldly knowledge is not considered real knowledge as it is relative and, therefore, never permanent or lasting. If, for example, a person was to get a degree in mathematics and then some time later take on some other type of work where that knowledge of mathematics is not utilised, then after some time she or he would forget most of the mathematics she or he had learned.

Spiritual knowledge or knowledge of the soul (*atma jinana*) can never be lost because it is infinite and unchanging. Upon realizing or knowing one's soul or *atman*, a person becomes the knower of spiritual knowledge and, because it is unchanging, it is known as *satya* or truth, and truth is Brahma. Brahma is the source of both worldly and spiritual knowledge and so those who know Brahma transcend time, place and person and become established in knowledge, truth, bliss and immortality.

Sadhana and svadhyaya give wisdom and spiritual knowledge. Svadhyaya, the reading of spiritual texts, gives *atma jinana* because its wisdom is not limited to time, place or person. It is unchanging and relevant in all circumstances and ages. Only specific books are recognized as giving this spiritual wisdom. In Ananda Marga, they are *Ananda Sutram* and *Subhasita Samgraha*. Also *Ananda Vacanamrtam* and *Namami Krsna Sundaram* are good sources of svadhyaya.

> *"Svadhyaya: the study, with proper understanding, of scripture and philosophical books:...The philosophical books and scripture of Ananda Marga are* Ananda Sutram *and* Subhasita Samgraha *(all parts) respectively."*

In these svadhyaya books the sadhaka will find the answers to the many questions which are needed for his or her spiritual progress. This invaluable knowledge removes many of the obstacles and dangers to the sadhaka on the spiritual path. Just as action is important for the expression of samskaras and producing certain qualities, similarly, a proper understanding of spirituality is vital. For example, the more we progress the more conspicuous the influences of *avidyamaya* (that is, the *pashas* and *ripus* — anger, fear, lust, aversion, doubt, etc.) become and the more critical the restraints and observances of Yama and Niyama become. Knowledge of this and other aspects of spirituality are vital for progress.

> *"If you feel the path is not pushing you then you should be more and more strict in morality."*

Daily svadhyaya instills in us spiritual ideas and inspiration which create spiritual desires and feelings. These created samskaras must eventually get expressed, so gradually our worldly life changes to express these spiritual feelings. If the mind is tied down to worldly thoughts, even during our sadhana, then at least by doing svadhyaya regularly, the vicious circle can be broken with spiritual thoughts.

"While moving towards Him do not neglect the world or the path of action. Although devotion is the most essential aid to help one to attain the Supreme stance, yet knowledge and action are very important. Without them, the possibility of downfall cannot be ruled out. Yet for the sadhaka, devotion is the highest quality."

Sadhana is very important for true knowledge because it gives deep insight and intuition. One can read the same svadyaya book many times over the years and always find new meaning in it. This is because our sadhana has given us greater perception of spiritual truths. Through regular sadhana and svadhyaya, we can attain wisdom.

"For intellectuals, spiritual progress is always delayed and the reason is this—that their intellectual body goes on increasing but for lack of apexed mentality, the Goal remains far away. But when the intellectual body is highly enlarged, it is sure to become one with the Macrocosm (God). For spiritual aspirants, this type of intellectual progress may be meaningless; it may be treated as superfluous. But for the human society as a whole this type of intellectual progress cannot be discouraged and must not be discouraged; rather it should be encouraged."

Knowledge based on personal spiritual experience is also of great benefit to the spiritual aspirant. By His grace alone, I was given spiritual experiences which cemented my faith and conviction in Him and His teachings. What was once merely bookish knowledge became a personal experience which I could truly understand. I still remember the feeling I had after one experience which lingered on for days. I experienced such great bliss in sadhana and such great feelings of love outside of sadhana that I even had to restrain myself from hugging a prison guard. I astonished a visitor by telling her I was quite happy to stay in jail for the entire duration of my 16 year sentence, such was the contentment and bliss that Baba was gracing me with. From that point onwards I have always given a lot of importance to my spiritual practices. *Baba Krpahi Kevalam.*

Mahapurusa, Bhagavan Baba is omnipresent. Past, present and future, subtle or crude, are all known to him. No other being, no matter how realized, has infinite knowledge like Bhagavan.

Although His worldly education was limited to that of an accounts clerk at a railway station in a small town in rural India, Baba could write and speak fluently any language of the world. When He was first taken to court to make His plea He was asked what language He would like to conduct his hearing in. (Due to the large number of languages spoken in India, changes are made to the language used in court to accommodate the accused.) To the astonishment of the court, Baba said that He knew over two hundred languages and asked what language *they* would like Him to speak in.

When a Margii asked Baba how He knew so many languages He said, "I know all the languages of the world by the grace of God."

"..in the realm of Dharma there should be clear-cut injunctions in the form of dharma shastra (scriptural treatise) and simultaneously there must be a strict guardian who during his lifetime guides himself as well as others according to those scriptural injunctions. After his demise, he will live forever in his teachings, which, although given for a particular age, will become a code of conduct for all time."

Baba can speak on any topic and sound like He has specialized in it for the whole of His life. For example when He speaks on geography about a particular mountain and its rivers, he will go into such detail about all the physical features of that area that one would think he must have visited that place personally. Baba can choose any language and describe its origin and how it came to its present form. Considering that He was a simple railway clerk, it seems incredible, virtually impossible, that any one person could have such knowledge. In a word, he must be omniscient.

Once Baba was travelling on a train to DMC. A politician and writer were sitting nearby and asked Baba what His profession was. Baba smilingly replied, "I write articles."

The man asked, "In what language do you write?"

Baba replied, "I write in all languages of the world."

"And on which subjects do you write?" asked the man.

"I write on all subjects. What is the meaning of Suhurta?"

The man was surprised that Baba knew his name and replied that he did not know its meaning. Baba spent the next 45 minutes explaining the man's name in many different languages.

A devotee was walking with Baba. Another devotee approached them and told Baba he had some good news. The first Ananda Marga school had just been opened. Baba said that in the future, schools will be established all over the world. The first devotee laughed. Baba asked why he was laughing and the devotee replied that the organization had only 40 workers, so it was impossible for the schools to become international so Baba must be joking. Baba smiled and said that it was not a joke, but a time would come when our schools would be in every part of the world. And, of course now, many years later, it is a fact that Ananda Marga schools exist all over the world. Many times Baba has foretold future events.

> *"Those who overact at the least provocation loose their power of judgment. One's internal power is determined by the degree of control one has over one's nerve cells. A person who cannot tolerate even a single provocative word obviously has no control over the nerves. He will never be able to do anything great because his self-confidence is easily shattered. One must develop the power of tolerance."*

Baba's omniscience means that He knows our every thought and deed. I have experienced this personally. After I received a pardon for wrongful imprisonment and was released from jail, I went to see my beloved Baba for the first time after having been a Margii for twelve years. In that time, some inferiority complexes had developed in my mind. I wondered if Baba really wanted to see me because every time in the past that I had tried to see Him my efforts had been blocked. When I finally did visit Him, He mocked my foolish doubts by making it appear that it was *me* who did not want to see *Him*.

When Baba got into His car to go on field walk, He put His hand out to me as I stood in front of His car window. Baba motioned for me to get in and sit with Him, but I did not understand what His hand motion meant. So I just did namaskar to Him. Baba said some nice words to me and left.

Then twice, after returning from field walk, after getting out of His car and doing those sweet, penetrating Namaskars to everyone present, Baba turned to me and made a hand gesture. Each time I did not know what they meant and just did Namaskar in reply to Him. And each time, I was told afterwards that Baba was asking how I was, was everything fine? I kicked myself each time for missing out on the opportunity to talk and be with Him.

After I did not reply to His last gesture regarding my health, Baba turned to His Personal Assistant and asked him. "Why doesn't Narada speak to me?"

Another doubt I had while going to see Baba was whether He appreciated the suffering I had experienced and the sacrifices I had made while in jail. Baba's standard was very high and there were others who had been in jail longer and suffered more, so I wondered if He thought much of what I had been through. This thought was more intellectual than from the heart but from time to time it came up, even though I did not like it for I knew that a true devotee should not do things with any expectation of praise from the Guru. It is a privilege to serve Him and to make sacrifices for Him—that is the reward and nothing else. As Baba writes:

"I will do exactly as He wants, I will color my mind with His color, and I will not think whether that will bring joy to me or not. Let Him be pleased...that is my only wish." This is the highest stage of devotion.

and:

It is a fact that the force of Avidya disturbs a spiritualist more than it disturbs an ordinary person. Various situations arise in life such as material difficulties, family unrest, abundant wealth, tremendous reputation, accute financial distress or extreme humiliation. Sadhakas will have to bravely confront these mundane situations as a test. They must never think in terms of retreat, it would be fatal, for the Avidya force would stab them as soon as their backs were turned.

One divine night at Lake Gardens, Baba came out for field walk. The atmosphere was romantic with night lights shining on Baba, giving an added radiance to His already radiant presence.

Just before He got into His car, Baba stopped and said in English,

"I would like to invite you all to attend a festival of light. This light is both within and without and I would like to invite you to attend it permanently."

Everyone was struck with wonder and delight at Baba's sudden burst of inspiration, and in English, too. Suddenly I found myself thanking Baba for what He had just said. Baba stopped and tilted His head forward with hand behind His divine ear, as if to say, "What was that you said?" Then He looked straight at me with deep love and appreciation and said, "And I thank you."

Immediately I knew that He was thanking me for what I had been through in jail and before. Such a strong wave of love came with those magic words, "and I thank you." As the words rang in my mind, Baba got into His car (with everyone else seeming to be unaware of what he had just said to me) and drove off, leaving me melting in love and ecstasy.

If we take one step towards Him, He takes three towards us...if not many more. Baba loves us for every little thing we do for Him, regardless of whether He shows it or not, although what we do is nothing compared to what He is doing for us every second of our lives. And mostly we fail to realize or appreciate these things He does. But such is His love and our ignorance.

It is only through proper sadhana that we can develop the intuition to understand so many parts of His liila.

One day Baba was talking about human psychology. He said it is not necessary to read a lot of books. When you do spiritual practices, eventually you will understand people. He mentioned that people with very thick skin often have a criminal mentality.

One Dada said, "But Baba, I have thick skin. What should I do?" Baba laughed and told him that if he did more sadhana, his skin would become thin. Baba went on to say that many people are what we call *shuchibai* or picky. They are always saying, "Don't do this," and "Don't touch that." Baba said that these people's minds are full of dirt, and that is why they think everything is dirty. He told this story:

Once a devotee of Rama passed by a tree and heard a bird singing in its branches. He heard the bird singing, "Ram, Sita, Dasharath" (Sita was Rama's wife, Dasharath his father). He felt happy that the bird was singing the Lord's name.

Then a Muslim man passed by the same tree. He heard the bird singing, "Allah, Khoda, Hazrat". He felt glad that even the birds were singing the Islamic praises.

Then a boy came by. He was thinking that no one liked him because he was only a lowly waiter at a hotel, serving onion and garlic to everyone. But then he heard the bird singing, "Garlic, onion, ginger," and felt happy.

Next a wrestler came by. He had heard that if one does a lot of physical exercise his brain will become dull. But then he heard the bird in the tree. It was singing, "Push-ups, sit-ups, knee-bends".

Baba laughed heartily and said, "You see, the bird was singing only bird song. But each, according to his own psychology, heard what he wanted to hear."

"No matter what stratum of life you find yourself in, if you love the Great, if you try to move towards Him, your insignificance will expand into greatness...If you adopt the reverse approach, that is, if you say, "I am so insignificant. Let me first remove my smallness, then I will proceed towards the Great. This is a huge psychological blunder."

Baba's mind, being one with Cosmic mind, knows past, present and future. About the future, He has said many things, including that when He leaves this planet the skeleton of Sadvipra Samaja would have been completed. We will have to fill in the detail ourselves.

In the much distant future, Baba says the human body will become smaller and thinner, but the head will become larger to cope with increased psychic expansion. On that point, Baba said that in places such as Germany, England, Bengal, and North America where intellectual development is greatest, the people have a lot of problems with their eyes and teeth—many of them have to wear glasses or false teeth. This is due to the pressure created by an expanding cranium, and not due to over use of eyes through reading.

Baba has also said that when the Earth gets overcrowded, people will fly to other planets to live. And when people wish to travel in the future, they will be able to leave their bodies in body 'banks,' send their brain to their destination, and when they reach there, take another body from a body bank.

Baba has said that in the future, as reproductive technology develops and more babies are produced in the test tube, our reproductive capacity will diminish. However the psychological urge to reproduce will always be there as it is inherent in the Comic mind, so we will go on reproducing through other means like test tubes.

Baba has said that only a few *vrttis* (mental propensities), in groups together, go to make up one's gender. He then did a demonstration. Baba waved His hand up and down in front of one Dada and then told those present that they will notice certain feminine features developing in that Dada. Apparently, Baba had said (many years back) that in the future, there will develop a problem of people wanting to change their sex. As people change their nature and develop the desire to do things which are natural to the opposite sex, the change in the predominance of certain vrttis will cause hormonal changes which are reflected in the body. For example, women doing heavy physical work, which is more suited to men's stronger bodies, develop more facial hair and the male hormones in them develop more to cope with the physical work.

Baba's worldly knowledge is clear to us. There are so many examples of His massive contribution in the areas of intellect and culture. His spiritual knowledge is even deeper, but it would be absurd and impossible to even try to explain a little of it, since it is beyond the mind and words. Only through personal intuitional experience can one appropriate or gain any of His spiritual knowledge.

> *"The most dangerous complex in the spiritual sphere is the superiority complex...Those suffering from a superiority complex find it impossible to withdraw the mind from its objects and, to their frustration, find that the mind easily slips away from its point of concentration. They will never be able to surrender such a mind to Paramapurusa ."*

6
Vaeragya:
Detachment

Vaeragya is the last of the qualities of Bhagavan. It means renunciation. Vaeragya does not mean suppression, nor does it necessarily mean giving up worldly possessions—especially family and society. Vaeragya means to be in the state where the mind feels indifferent or unattached to any objects or entity.

> *"The practice whereby detachment in developed for finite objects, that is, the discipline whereby the mind is not influenced by the attraction of worldly objects is Vaeragya sadhana."*

Bhagavan Shrii Shrii Anandamurti certainly possessed Vaeragya. On the physical plane, He owned very little for His personal use. Baba's clothes were always very clean and neat, but never aristocratic. His office was always simple but adequate for His work, thus never placing a burden upon others.

Baba's mental detachment was easy to observe. There was a very rich Margii, who came to Ananda Marga in its early days. At this time, this Margii was also very immoral. One day he went to see Baba with seven *lakhs* (700,000) rupees to give to Baba, thinking that Baba would be very pleased with him.

When he met Baba, he gave Baba the money in a bag. But Baba knew about his motives and threw the money out onto the streets. The man thought that Baba did not know what was in the bag and went running out onto the streets to collect the money. In the meantime, Baba locked the door.

When the man returned to Baba's door and knocked, Baba would not let him in saying that because he would rather run after money than Him he could stay out.

Vaeragya means detachment or renunciation of worldly desires. This is different from the suppression of desires which is just as bad, if not worse, than the expression of them. While both lead to crudification, suppression leads to perversion as well. Suppression leads to obsession which leads to perversion.

Vaeragya also does not mean avoiding worldly or family responsibilities by running off to the jungles or mountains. Rather, it means to live in the world but in a detached way, having neither attraction nor aversion to the world (because both are caused by *Avidyamaya*). It is only when we have this detachment, along with *viveka* or proper discrimination, that we can advance to higher states of spirituality, including the development of true love.

> *"Seeing how dearly you love your children, a* mayavadin *[one who sees the world as illusion] will say, 'Be careful! You are about to fall into the snare of attachment. Remember, this relative world is just an illusory prison.' To such a negative statement a genuine Ananda Margii will say with robust optimism, 'Of course I will love my children with all my heart and through sadhana expand this love to its greatest or unlimited extent. Let this love which was confined to one child be extended to all children. By taking the hearts of all parents within one's own heart, one realizes that every child is worthy of this love.'"*

Once while I was in jail, Baba came to me in a very strange way. But in doing so He gave me an understanding of spiritual detachment and love. For many days, He had me in a high state, only to eventually take it away and leave me acutely depressed for three months. Life seemed so dry and meaningless without spiritual love. The following poem was inspired by this experience with Him:

> Love is that which takes the rough edge off life
> And gives new hope and inspiration
> Love is not of the body, nor the mind: true love is of the soul
> When it awakes it swells upwards,
> Bursting out from the heart
> It injects a perpetual feeling of beauty, peace and goodness
> For true love is pure benevolence and altruism,
> Flavoured in the sweetest nectar.
> There is no selfish gain involved
> The true love becomes the maker of the Beloved
> The Beloved's happiness and sorrows are
> The lovers' happiness and sorrow
> All things and considerations take second place behind the Beloved
>
> And such an intimately secret affair it is
> Too pure and profound for words to speak or describe.
> Only the lover really knows just how real and fulfilling it is.
> While true love may cause pain, it is the most sweet pain.
> In Love the lover is lost in the Beloved,
> Intoxicated with Love's ecstacy and bliss,
> Nothing else exists or matters
> In true Love one experiences the meaning of life

After being convicted, I felt like I had been thrown into a deep, dark hole and told, "Now, let's see you get out if you can." While I felt alone and helpless, I also felt Baba come to my side and given me strength. I mentally said to Him that only He could get me out of jail and I knew, when the time was right, He would bring me out. That day I surrendered my fate to Him. I never asked Him to get me out— that was in His hands. I just concerned myself with following the Sixteen Points to the best of my ability, given my circumstances—and this was my biggest clash rather than whether or not, or when I would get out. Baba had graced me with detachment about my release. Later I realized how much He had blessed and graced me while in prison.

> *"If Parama Purusa wants to forgive someone, to remove their afflictions, He does so indirectly by inspiring them to perform some good deeds. But everyone should remember in this case that one is bound to reap the good consequences of good deeds and the bad consequences of bad deeds. One can develop the capacity to bear sufferings at the time of hardship by the grace of Parama Purusa: it is indeed a great blessing from Him."*

Indeed as I look back, I can see Baba's grace in so many ways. While a prisoner was bashing me over the head with a cricket stump, instead of pain, I felt only a slight pressure. It was not until I saw blood on my shirt that I realized some serious damage had been done.

During a 150-day hunger strike, He gave me so much strength that, at times, I had to pretend that I was weaker than I really felt because the authorities would have thought that I was secretly taking food—and would then have sent me from the hospital back to jail. In the last week of the hunger strike, when the doctor warned us of permanent organ damage due to protein deficiency (we were only drinking fruit juice) if we did not end our fast at the end of the week, our demands were met and so I could end the fast and avoid physical danger. The list goes on and on.

When neither a blade of grass nor a huge galaxy can move without His grace, how can we ever forget or doubt His hand in our lives?

Due to ignorance we sometimes blame him for our sufferings, forgetting that it is because of our past misdeeds that they occur. Even God has to abide by Prakrti's laws when He enters her creation. If we break her law, we suffer and we have only ourselves to blame. We must take responsibility for the situations in which we find ourselves. Baba said:

> Sadhakas' sufferings are caused by the samskaras which they created themself. At the time of suffering, a sadhaka should reproach himself for his past misdeeds and refrain from evil actions in order to avoid more suffering in the future...You must not find fault with others because of your samskaras, which are merely the reactions caused by your own mistakes and misbehaviour.

While this is the attitude which we should take to our own sufferings, it is not the attitude to take towards the sufferings of others. Once a man remarked to Baba that others suffer because of their samskaras. Baba became angry and said, "Don't think about that. That is the duty of Prakrti. Your duty is to serve!"

"At the time of great difficulty, when agony swells people's hearts and they are unable to restrain themselves, the sufferers should say only one thing to Parama Purusa. 'Oh my Paramapurusa, the life of my life, give me the strength to endure.'"

In the past, Tantrik Gurus would make their disciples do hard penance and *tapah* (sacrifice) for many years before giving them initiation. A disciple had to be pure, surrendered and detached. Fortunately, for most of us, Baba said that suffering humanity cannot wait for us to be ready, therefore He is giving us initiation now, and then giving us much struggle and clash after initiation. He gives us this clash through our personal spiritual practices and organizational work. That is why, at times, things seem a little crazy or illogical, but that is His liila and method for our purification and elevation. We have to learn detachment and faith.

Rather than being attached to Baba, we are usually attached to things of the world: people, work, pride, possessions. food, etc. But He wants us to direct our attachment to Him rather than to the world.

One Dada was standing outside Baba's house at Lake Gardens when he was called in to see Baba. Baba asked if he knew why he had been called and not the other workers who were also waiting outside. Dada did not know. Baba explained that all the others were thinking about worldly things—food, money, people, work, gossiping and so on—whereas only he was thinking of Baba. So Baba only wanted to see him.

Baba has expressed to some devotees His hurt that they are thinking about other people and things while He is constantly thinking about them. Like a jealous lover, He waits in pain for us to return the constant loving attention He gives us.

Along with Baba's detachment is His humility and sense of humor. In the early days of Ananda Marga, a new Margii had just received initiation from an acharya. He was so inspired and excited that he rushed out onto the streets to tell everyone about Baba and sadhana. The first man he met stopped and listened to everything the new Margii had to say. He agreed to go back with him and meet his Acharya. To the surprise of the Acarya and embarrassment of the new Margii, the person he had brought back was Baba Himself!

> *"The greatest thing people should learn from Shiva is straightforwardness and simplicity, along with unflinching devotion to duty."*

One devotee was washing Baba's hands. This was his duty. He had an inferiority complex because he was illiterate. He said to Baba, "Baba, everyone in Ananda Marga is intellectual." Baba replied, "Yes, that is true, only you and I are illiterate." Hearing this, the devotee dropped his pitcher of water and went into samadhi.

"It is because of samskaras that the introversive momentum is rare in the average human mind. The sensuous desires of Avidya continue to infiltrate into every thought process. Such a situation continues for a long time in a sadhaka's life."

When Baba was a high school student, the day came when the results of the Higher School Certificate exams were printed in the newspaper. As soon as the newspaper came out Baba's friends eagerly looked for their names as well as Baba's. If one's name does not appear, then that indicates failure. When His friends could not find His name, they became very concerned and rushed to tell Him. Baba was at home, totally unconcerned and detached about His results. They found Him calmly cleaning His teeth. They very nervously told Him that they could not find His name. Baba told them to look at the tenth name in the list—that was where His name was.

Baba's whole life is filled with examples of detachment. When He was working at the railways, He authorized His younger brother to draw His salary on His behalf and to give it to His mother. His mother would then give Him a small amount of 'pocket money' which He would use to serve the needy or to buy fruits and flowers for His mother.

When Baba was released from jail, there was great drama and excitement. He remained completely calm and detached saying that He was unconcerned when people criticized Him and He would remain equally detached from their praise.

While Baba was detached, His devotees are sometimes not so detached. Seeing His son, Kimsuk worried and miserable when Baba was in hospital, Baba reassured him saying, "Don't worry. You know I have taken some targets in my life. No matter what you may see happening to this body of mine, don't worry. I will fulfil those targets and then, and only then, will I leave this body. So don't you worry like this anymore."

The following is an interview Baba gave to "India Today", August 1978, when He was released. It shows His tremendous detachment, amongst other things!

Baba almost never spoke directly to the public or the media, but in this rare case He agreed to give written answers to a reporters' questions.

Q: How do you feel about the verdict of the High Court? While millions of your followers the world over celebrated the day as " Victory of Dharma" you did not express any reaction and one of your followers explained that since you are *Nirbbikar* (passionless) you received this news coolly. Is it a fact you never react to anything and if so why ?

Baba: Victory of Dharma is a natural phenomenon. Everything natural should be accepted with normal coolness.

Q: Your followers allege that you and your organization have been a victim of calculated malicious propoganda by a certain agency aimed at destroying your organization. Much damage has been caused to your organisation during the past seven years during which you were in jail. Now, if you are acquitted of all charges, how do you plan to remove misunderstanding from the public mind to re-establish your organization?

Baba: We will be doing our humanitarian duties with subjective approach and objective adjustment.

Q: Much confusion was created in the past because of lack of communication between you and the general public. Do you now think it is proper to have public contact so that the confusion does not persist? Why have you lived a secluded life in the past?

Baba: There is no necessity of my coming in public contact because actual social service is rendered by the workers of the organisation. I simply assist the workers.

Q: The speed with which Ananda Marga has spread in the west and attracted a large number of people, has created misgivings that it is being supported or sponsored by some foreign agencies. Moreover, your attack on the KGB and CBI in the past without mentioning the name of the CIA has added to the confusion. What have you to say to this allegation?

Baba: I do not know if CIA did any harm to Ananda Marga. If the same is brought to my notice with sufficient proof, I will certainly condemn them. I have got no weakness for any organization. Good people should always be supported and bad condemned in unambiguous language.

Q: It was alleged that you wanted to capture political power and establish Sadvipra Raj in the world. No doubt this was refuted in the court but at the same time the books referred to in the court during trial confirmed this view in which you have said, " Violence is the essence of life." How do you explain the fact?

Baba: What I said in the court is final. The word I use is "Sadvipra Samaj" and not "Sadvipra Raj." "Raj" [Kingdom] is a microscopic fraction of Samaj [Society]. My view regarding violence has already been clarified by me. It is not always Himsa. My interpretation of violence can co-exist with Ahimsa.

Q: Do you have any political ambitions? Do you feel that unless corruption was removed, the society would not be of your liking? And how do you want to establish that kind of society unless you take an active part in politics, is it possible?

Baba: I have got no politcal ambition. I have propounded the theory of Prout for the welfare of human society. This theory will be materialize by those who love it.

Q: What is your opinion about democracy?

Baba: Democracy can be successful only where the following essential factors are present at least amongst 51 percent of the voters: morality, literacy and socio-economic-political consciousness. Otherwise it is an instrument to befool the public.

"There cannot be any peace, any happiness, any beautitude, until the aspirant comes in tactual contact with the Supreme Stance."

7
Conclusion:
Surrender is the final word

"The path of spirituality is beset with numerous obstacles."

I have tried to explain the concept of Bhagavan and, using stories and experiences, show that Baba is indeed Bhagavan. This attempt to explain Bhagavan is not to convince anyone, but rather to inspire those who have already realized Baba's Divinity. The concept of Bhagavan is not one to be understood by intellectual analysis but through psycho-spiritual experiences and realisation.

According to spiritual science, a Guru can only take His or Her disciple to that height which He or She has attained Him or Herself—and no higher. Bhagavan or Sadguru has attained the highest state and so can give Nirvikalpa Samadhi to others. Only Bhagavan can do this. Bhagavan is Divine at birth and therefore does not need to pursue spiritual practices in order to attain enlightenment. Any Guru who has had to do sadhana for enlightenment cannot give Nirvikalpa Samadhi and therefore is not Bhagavan. Baba has given Nirvikalpa Samadhi to many of His devotees.

There were more than 10,000 people at DMC in Ranchi. Baba was explaining that if Maya was gone, everybody would go into *savikalpa samadhi*—everybody would merge into that liberated state. Just after His explanation, He called one avadhuta to him.

Conclusion

Baba said, "Stand before me. Now what are you seeing?"

With his face towards the sadhakas, the avadhuta said, "Baba, I am seeing sadhakas."

Then Baba said again after a pause, "Now what are you seeing?" Dada said, "Baba, I am seeing only You. All have become Baba."

After another pause, Baba asked, "What are you seeing now?" Dada replied, "Baba, I am seeing that there is only one Baba!"

Then Baba clapped three times and the avadhuta immediately fell into *nirvikalpa samadhi*. Baba said, "You know, I can give this state to all the creatures of the universe at one time. But do you know, if I give this state the neutrality of this universe will be disturbed. So I will give all of you this state gradually and in time."

Only by following Bhagavan's directives can we come to understand Him. The more our minds are expanded and surrendered, the more we may realize His greatness. I say 'may' because His Grace is also required before we can realize anything about Him. To a crude person, Baba is just an ordinary man, but to His devotees, He is Divinity incarnate. As soon as we stop trying to sincerely follow His directives, our appreciation of His greatness wavers and downfall is quite possible. When the Lord of the Universe is calling for us, how can we not follow Him? As one devotee said to a crowd of businessmen, "You fools, the Lord of the Universe has come! Run, take initiation, Taraka Brahma is here!" Yes, run. Throw yourself into His great mission without further delay. Do not doubt. Be faithful and you will be successful.

"One who ideates on the Supreme Entity while engaged in individual and social endeavour, establishes a happy co-relation between Bhaeravii Shakti and Cognitive Faculty. Such a person will never degenerate even though his or her cherished Supreme Goal may not be fully realised. The main factor is the clear awareness of one's goal. One's greatness is determined by one's goal." "He who loves me, I snatch all his possessions, and he ever remains with me, and I become his slave."

> "He who loves me, I snatch all his possession, and he ever remains with me, and I become his slave."

> "Just as a child never has to think about itself—its parents think about its well-being—similarly, you should not concern yourself about your own needs. Let Parama Purusa worry about that while you carry on your duty fearlessly and cheerfully."

Jumping into His nectarian flow, we drift along in His infinite ocean of intoxicating bliss.

"Really blessed is he who attained complete surrender unto Him, like a piece of salt which went to measure the depth of the ocean—but a momentous jerk and an attraction occurred and that piece of salt was lost, none knows where."

Just as we can only have one *Ista*, (goal, or Baba) we can only have one *Adarsha* (Ideology). To try and mix other systems or philosophies will only weaken us and we will always suffer confusion, frustration and other clashes between our ego's desires and His. Baba wants our full commitment—nothing less. We have to surrender our doubts, fears and attachments and jump into His loving arms. When we surrender, we find that the things that once held us back now seem superficial and unimportant. What's more, things which once seemed like sacrifices to us now become joyful. We get to experience Him and as our caring parent, He takes care of all our (real) needs, including our worldly needs. Although now they are much less than before.

Ananda Marga is great for its sadhana and service, but greatest for sacrifice and surrender. Baba says we should not want to have an easy life but rather we should desire to be a fine person and that "the greatest thing in life is to have an ideology."

CONCLUSION 89

Baba made this comment on ideology to a doctor in the hospital in which He stayed in early 1990 when He was seriously ill with a diabetes complaint. While He was there many of the doctors and nurses fell in love with Him, as have many non-Margiis who have had contact with His Divine personality.

In the early days of Ananda Marga a group of non-Margiis approached Baba for guidance, saying that Baba loves them as well as Margiis so He should tell them something.

Baba sent a message to them saying that they should always remember the world *Bhavisca'* and that they can use it as a mantra. The word is made up of the words *Bhagavan* (God), *vinay* (modesty), *samyama* (self-restraint and control) and *caritra* (good conduct).

Baba explained that they should always remember that God (Bhagavan) exists and to act accordingly as per the other parts of the mantra He gave: modesty, self-restraint and good conduct. In this way Baba showed the importance of spirituality to all, including non-Margiis.

As a Neo-Humanist Baba loves all, including plants and animals. Once while in hospital, He refused to take insulin because it was an extract from animal pancreas. Baba told His doctor, "I want that not a single living creature should ever say that, because of P.R. Sarkar, my life was destroyed. Maybe at some time I have unknowingly harmed some creature, but knowingly I have never done so."

"Bear in mind that you have a duty towards—indeed, you owe a debt to... every creature of this universe. But towards you, no one has any duty—from others nothing is due."

While He loves all, regardless of who they are or what they do, to love Him sincerely we must do His sadhana. But sadhana involves more than may appear on the surface. While it is important to know He loves us, it's more important to know we love Him!

There is a rather interesting and very important message told in one story that I think all of Baba's devotees should know.

Some time just before Baba was imprisoned when many Margiis were leaving Ananda Marga, there was one Dada who became very perturbed and confused as to what to do. He was thinking, "Why are all these good sadhakas leaving and saying such bad things about Ananda Marga and Baba?" He was wondering who was right and what he should do.

All-knowing Baba was in Patna and Dada was in Calcutta. Baba told His PA to send for Dada. When Dada received the message, he left for Patna. As he entered Baba's room, Baba asked how he was, but Dada gave no reply. Baba told him to come on a field walk with Him.

Normally no one speaks to Baba unless He speaks first, but Dada was restless and asked Baba, "Baba, will those avadhutas come back? Why have they left? They were such good sadhakas."

"Do you know what sadhana is?" Baba asked. Dada did not answer. Baba then went on to explain that there are two types of paths: the Vedic path and the Tantrik path. On the Vedic path, there is nothing but external worship, such as prayer, and no importance is placed on the Guru or on sadhana. On the Tantrik path there is internal Sadhana and the Guru is all-important. Here *mukti* or *moksa* is guaranteed—not like on the Vedic path. Here the oath and surrender is needed. When one takes the oath at initiation it's as if the Guru is now taking hold of your wrist and pulling you to Him. The Guru is now pulling you on towards victory.

But when the sadhaka starts to offer everything to the Guru, when they do mental Guru Puja—surrender to Guru—the disciple or devotee takes hold of the guru's wrist and it is now that real progress starts.

This relationship of closeness and surrender to the Guru is very, very important. Without a close relationship with the Guru, there is nothing. I see this to mean that when only the Guru is pulling you to Him, the sadhaka is doing the sadhana of convenience so to speak—only doing what suited the sadhaka's personal desires and feelings. There is no real surrender or effort to follow His wishes. The sadhaka was always trying to fit the Guru's wishes into his or her own wishes and enjoying the path accordingly.

But where there is the Guru-devotee bond of closeness, the sadhaka is trying to fit his or her desires into the Guru's. This means following the systems, disciplines and organization which the Guru has created. One may not like some of them, but because it pleases Him, they are followed. This sentiment of surrendering one's desires to follow Him is called *prapati*. And the sentiment of closeness which is experinced is expressed according to our samskaras. That is, either one loves Him "as a mother loves her child, a wife her husband, a servant his master, or as love between friends." This is purely an internal and personal thing. It is a very sweet and blissful concept, but only those who practice it can know how intoxicatingly Divine it is.

"Try to awaken your latent devotional sentiment. It will come to you if you wish. Once the devotion is awakened you shall get divine mercy without doubt."

After the relationship is established, the Guru gives several tests with the last one being the hardest, most dangerous and important. Regardless of whether or not one 'passes' other tests that the Guru might give, it is this one that ultimately counts. It is here that the Guru creates such circumstances that one begins to doubt Him.

If one fails this test, then it is as if the disciple has let go of the Guru's hand, but because the Guru is all-powerful, He still pulls and guides the disciple towards Him. However, if one now stops doing His sadhana, the *tamasik* or *avidyamaya* forces can very easily take hold and so the disciple starts to mentally say, "Go away Guru. Leave my life, I want nothing to do with You !" It is now that the Guru has no other choice but to let go of the disciple's hand and the disciple fails. The higher the desciple has gone, the farther she or he falls and it will usually take many lifetimes before the desciple will develop the desire for sadhana again.

Doubting the guru or doubting the path is one of the three dangers on the spiritual path—living in the past and comparing yourself with others are the other two, Baba has explained. The danger with 'living in the past' or having attachments for the past, is that it can bring up old samskaras which will distract or destroy us. We can learn from the past, but to live in the past is dangerous. As Baba says:

> You have to forget all your past deeds—all your tales of glory and ignominy, right from the memorable moment you start moving on the path of sadhana. Don't look back. You have no eyes behind. Indispensable as it is to be cautious and careful, lest your self-created tornado propelling you forward does not dash you down to the ground, in order to ensure your safe journey ahead, throw back a cursory glance and no more.

The danger with comparing oneself to others is that superiority or inferiority complexes are created. We may think, "I am a better sadhaka than him," or "she is a better worker than me." In both cases the ego is affected and this can lead to one's downfall.

Baba allows sadhakas to experience different things according to what is best for their progress. Baba likens the spiritual journey to a train trip. Two people may be going to the same destination but only one has the blinds open and gets to enjoy the many views on the journey. Both people ultimately reach the same destination.

So to compare other sadhakas experiences on the spiritual path with our own is meaningless and vain. Our only concern should be our relationship with Him. The only thing we can gain from others is their good examples to follow or bad conduct to avoid. But these should not be seen as a gauge of our own progress. Our progress is determined by our love and surrender to Him.

Another danger with comparing oneself with others is that if a sadhaka is going through difficult times and begins to compare his or her path with another seemingly 'happier' path, there can be a temptation to leave their path. For example, a sadhaka may feel attraction for a non-spiritual life. This can occur after comparing one's path with anothers. Once we have made a commitment to one particular path, we should concern ourselves only with that and not allow our minds to indulge in comparing it with other paths.

This same problem can also develop from living in the past. We may think during a period of much clash, "I was much happier before joining Ananda Marga. Maybe I should leave as it only brings me troubles."

Many people have foolishly left their path (and Ananda Marga) because of difficulties, thinking they can find happiness in another path. These comparisons can also create jealousy and resentment, making us want or think we should have what others have. However, the Lord gives us exactly what He feels is best for our growth and so to think otherwise is foolish and even dangerous. It crudifies our ideation and leads us from the path. Baba explained:

> "Even while remaining in this exalted state, sometimes it happens that the mind of the devotee runs after materiality for a short while... For instance, a poor person at the sight of the wealth of a rich man may be tempted to think, "If I had that much wealth,

I could have rendered greater service to the society and to Parama Purusa.

...These desires for the acquisition of more material wealth, for more scholarship and eloquence, are certainly distortions of the smooth flow of a devotee's mind. Perhaps there is no defect regarding one's goal, but the defect lies in the psychic movement in the world of ideation, because one must work according to the capacity which Parama Purusa has already bestowed—this is what He expects us to do."

And.....

"You should always think in terms of Ideology and collective interest and never in personal terms. Generally a stroke of difficulty or a blow to personal prestige or position diverts one's attention towards oneself, and the great Ideology is forgotten. This feeling may be either positive or negative but it preoccupies a large portion of the mind and thereby creates too much self-consciousness which makes one lazy and vocal. One then chats about oneself, one's difficulties, and one's relations with persons surrounding oneself and incidents. One loses balance of mind. In short, one then thinks all the time about oneself forgetting one's Ideology and task."

For sadhana, Baba said only two things are needed, "implicit faith and sincerity. Arouse these two things through your will power and victory is yours—it must be."

Will power is gained through discipline or by following the 16 Points. Constantly thinking or acting in a certain way changes our hormonal secretions which in turn changes our feelings and desires.

For example, while once it may have seemed an inconvenience to take a half-bath, after some time of practice, it becomes uncomfortable if we don't take one. Our mind is strengthened which produces willpower. It's good to remember that our thoughts and actions determine our destiny. That is:

Thought= Action= Habit= Character= Destiny

Of all disciplines, sadhana gives us the most willpower and strength of mind. It is the key to following our path and to attaining Him. To understand and be able to use microvita, Baba says that we have to do more sadhana. To become neo-humanists, He says we must do "austere sadhana." Indeed, Baba says we should miss out on food, sleep and bath before missing sadhana.

"The only way for the final removal of... afflictions is sadhana. That is why people should do meditation as much as possible. If sadhana is not done, then one's food, bath and sleep should also be given up. Similarly, whenever there is the opportunity and time, one must do Kiirtan, which is the most useful practice for sadhana."

But it must be good sadhana, done for His pleasure. Only then can we hope to gain real devotion and thus attain Him.

"Devotion is the life-force of a devotee, and without it nothing can be achieved. When the life-force leaves a person's body, death quickly follows. Similarly, if devotion is taken away from the devotees, they too will die. So, devotees always want to listen to topics of devotion—they do listen and they should listen."

What is devotion? Constant ideation on Him with the desire to serve selflessly to please only Him, is devotion. And how do we serve Him selflessly? Baba wrote that there are three ways to serve Him:

Physical Service: Here we selflessly serve His creation as an expression of Him and while we are serving we feel that is is He who is doing the service. We cannot do anything. Only by His grace can things happen or get done. Even if things do not get done, that is also His doing. But that is provided we have surrendered the vanity of doership to Him.

Even the feeling of pride that He has chosen us and not others to do His work must be surrendered. We can only witness and enjoy the bliss that comes with this surrendered ideation. If there is this vanity of doership in the action—ie. "I have achieved this, I have failed that..."—then this 'service', coming from Ahamtattva (small ego) does not please Parama Purusa. Baba writes that it also fails to inspire others and creates psychic disease like suppression.

"Everything is dancing in the rhythm of Parama Purusa. But people think, I am doing, I am giving, this was done by me, that was done by me, etc. Though people at this stage are moving in the path of sadhana, still there is some defect in them. Their minds do not inspire the minds of others; their minds do not touch the minds of others. They do not reach the sweetness of others' I-feelings, for they are too preoccupied with themselves. Their approach is defective; their path is not the path of Neo-Humanism."

While working and serving, our vrttis will want expression. This includes the crude *pashas* and *ripus*. Unless we have love or spiritual ideation and can then redirect our crude vrttis to Him, the only other recourse is to suppress them. Both expression and suppression of crude vrttis are degrading, however suppression is worse.

"If there is no love for the Supreme Entity, what will happen? Your work will be fruitless, and you will suffer from different psychic diseases such as frustration..."

When doing service, we must remember that we have the right to perform actions but not to their results. That is His concern. Work and serve with the utmost sincerity and ideation, but do not become attached to the outcome. That will cause either pride or disappointment and disillusionment.

Baba Krpahi Kevalam. What is Krpa or Grace? Action + Surrender = Grace. That is, be tirelessly active in trying to follow His directives, but surrender the fruits of the actions to Him. Then grace will come. This applies to both our work and our sadhana. Of course grace can also come through a moment of intense love for Him.

Individuality thrives on Avidya and from Avidya it is born.

Psychic Service: This means kiirtan. When we do kiirtan, He goes to the place we are doing kiirtan and gets great joy. And so do we. Kiirtan is a great cleanser of the ego and its impurities and negativities. It makes us simple, happy and carefree with a synthetic approach to life. Ideally we should do kiirtan every time before sadhana, thus ensuring our Lord at least gets psychic pleasure from our spiritual practice. (He will not get pleasure from our sadhana if it is filled with worldly thoughts and desires.) The only person who Baba has said was a Neo-Humanist was Caetanaya Mahaprabhu, the person responsible for introducing kiirtan—and a constant practitioner of it.

>Instead of wasting their time in idle gossip, people should do kiirtan whenever they have time....When a large number of people do kiirtan....(their) concentrated physical and psychic force removes the accumulated sorrows and miseries of the material world.... Whenever the devotees do kiirtan in one place, Parama Purusa takes His seat on the throne of their hearts. He shifts His nucleus to that place....
>
>All obstacles and dangers are removed by collective kiirtan—flood, drought, famine, pestilence, earthquake and all such natural calamities can be averted if people do kiirtan with sincerity. Human miseries will be removed then and there....
>
>Kiirtan removes various psychic troubles also....which have already arrived, and troubles which have not yet come but there are forebodings.

Spiritual Service: This means sadhana, particularly *dhyana* (the sixth lesson of meditation). In proper dhyana, Baba gets direct pleasure and happiness. Our ideation becomes His reality. Here we can direct all our feelings and vrttis to Him without any negative reaction. Only in dhyana is there is no degeneration caused by the expression of our vrttis. It is called converting *pravrtti* (worldly desires) into *nivrtti* (desirelessness). This specifically relates to dhyana. As with physical and psychic service, spiritual service must he done with intense love. Otherwise Baba says that we are wasting our time. Of course we must also follow the prescribed system correctly—with correct posture, very straight back, and teeth and tongue in the correct position.

....If you do your sadhana for 10, 20 or 24 hours in a day, but there is no love for the Supreme Entity, what will happen? You will simply be misusing the time, abusing the time.

During meditation you should think that the entity on whom you are meditating is looking at you as His object. He is not your object. He sees whatever you are doing. This should be the psychology. He can never be your object. During meditation you should remember that when the Supreme Entity looks upon you, He sees you as his object. He is not your object, you are His object.

It is ironic that the Lord created this Universe to remove His loneliness, yet His creation has largely forgotten Him for the attractions and distractions of the world. What a crime! However, as soon as our mind is withdrawn inward and concentrated on Him, His eternal loneliness is removed—and the purpose of creation fulfilled.

My Lonely Beloved
(Esoteric Love)

I used to wait for Him—to come to me,
Until I realized He waits for me.
Waiting, waiting, my lonely Beloved waits only for me.
So I rush to embrace Him,
To merge and tearfully vow never to be separated again.
Like Radha and Krsna, we lovers love,
Caring and wanting nothing but each other;
And serving with such young romantic hearts.
But Maya gets jealous of me.
Skillfully I am distracted back to the external world,
Away from my Vrindavan and my lonely Beloved.
Forgetting Him, becoming deaf to His cries,

Maya's veil has made me numb to Him.
But love is stronger even than Maya,
And I run back into His waiting lonely arms.
He is always so happy to see me,
Because I am His only true love.
My love is all He desires of me.
So happy, blissful and satisfied he becomes,
And so do I.

—Narada Muni

The more we ideate and do sadhana and service in a selfless, loving way, the more pleasure Baba gets. This is *bhakti* or devotion. But bhakti alone is not enough. Baba says *jinana* (knowledge) and *karma* (action) are needed to give intensity to devotion. But these are aids to devotion and not superior to it. Karma is serving the Lord with one's body. Jinana is serving the Lord with one's mind. And bhakti is serving the Lord with one's heart. Baba is found in the heart of the loving devotee. For the devotees, all their knowledge and action become mere expressions of devotion, of their heart's love for Him.

For devotees, all actions are a part of their psycho-spiritual practice, whereas for *karmiis* actions are merely seen as actions. Those people whose actions are indistinguishable from devotion are true devotees.

Through devotion we can find and get Him. Remember Baba said He came to this planet to create devotion- everything else is ultimately an aid to the achievement of that end.

Educated, intelligent and clever people consider the path of devotion to be superior. Devotees, on the other hand, consider the paths of action and knowledge to be those of the fools.

Conclusion

Baba is always stressing the importance of our spiritual practices, but what is His sadhana? One Dada was talking to Baba and asked him mischievously,

"Baba, You taught us to do meditation, but I want to know what kind of meditation You do. I think I should do that also. It must be better than what You taught us."

Baba laughed and said, "So you want to do my meditation? Do you think you can do it ?"

Dada said, "Yes, of course Baba. I will try."

Baba replied, "All right then. I will tell you. First I sit like this (indicating lotus posture). Then I close my eyes and gather all my sons and daughters all over the world (extending His arms and sweeping them towards Himself), and mentally I look at each and every one of them. I see what they are doing, and how they are, if they are alright or if they need help. This is my dhyana. I meditate on you people. You may do it also, if you can."

Baba has given so many types of sadhana for sadhakas with different samskaras. It can be the highly colourful and very blissful Vishesh yoga, the powerful and courageous Kapalika sadhana, the very sweet and intimate Madhur Gosti sadhana, the personal and energising Microvita sadhana, or the blissful lessons of our Sahaj yoga, not to speak of those sadhanas known only to Baba and those concerned. It is said that He has sent sadhakas (not Margiis) to the Himalayas to do a special type of sadhana all day. This sadhana sends out vibrations to different parts of the world, raising the consciousness of the people there. Whatever sadhana one has, it has the capacity to take us to our goal of Parama Purusa. Provided of course that it is done properly with correct ideation and love, regularly and sincerely.

Without the strength of mind, detachment and ideation we gain from regular sadhana, nothing great can be achieved.

You should keep the mind cool and calm every moment. You should never react to any stimulus immediately although you must maintain proper knowledge about your environment. (You must be well-informed.)
To have a calm and cool mind, one needs spiritual practice. Therefore, whatever others may say, your daily spiritual practices should not be reduced or neglected. Without the strength of mind achieved by spiritual practice nothing great can be accomplished.

When sadhana is good, everything happens much more smoothly and effectively. Things get done because He is doing it, not the ego.

The sadhaka, the spiritual aspirant, must remember that spirituality is the mainstream of life and everything else is peripheral to it. With the inspiration from sadhana, you can go on working in the mundane, supramundane and psychic spheres.

Those people can be called intelligent who utilize every moment of their short life engaged in spiritual practice.

Because worldly work can be so engrossing, it is easy to forget the goal of life and the way to achieve it—through sadhana. But this is only more reason to be strict in our spiritual practices.

The only aim of life is spiritual practice—the realisation of the Supreme... People will have to conduct their lives in such such a way that their mundane duties are properly discharged without disturbing their spiritual practice, which is the goal of life... But human psychology is such that after performing worldly duties for awhile, people deviate from the main goal of life, sometimes so far that they tend to look upon their worldly duties only as a means of self-agrandisement. That is the moment of their downfall.

Sometime in 1965, a Dada was with Baba alone. Baba was in a happy mood. Dada told Baba that his sadhana was not going well.

Baba replied, "You go on and do more and more sadhana as it is your duty, and leave the result for me to take care of."

Baba asked, "Suppose you are waiting for a train and it is late, then how will you utilize the time?"

The devotee answered, "I will read the newspaper."

"What is the better alternative?" asked Baba.

"I can propagate our ideology and do pracar," he replied.

"Isn't there anything better you could do?" asked Baba.

The devotee felt quite close to Baba and replied jokingly, "I could eat peanuts."

Baba smiled and said he should utilize the available time by doing sadhana. The devotee rejected Baba's remarks saying it was impossible to do sadhana in a railway station because of the noisy environment.

Baba said, "You are so logical and never want to try."

Soon after that a situation arose when Dada's train was late, so he decided to follow Baba's advice and do sadhana, despite the noise. Because of his orange monk's uniform, the people in the station lowered their voices in respect and Dada had a quiet and deep sadhana.

Sometimes we feel His directives are impossible or impractical to follow, but if we surrender our limited minds and attachment to logic and "just do," then often we get a pleasant surprise—we get His grace.

"Love for the feeling of Ideology and oneness with the Propagator makes one invincible, impregnable. One becomes like pure gold."

8
Postscript:
Baba's Departure

It was Sunday afternoon, October 21st, 1990. Baba had been ill with a variety of ailments, but now he was back from the hospital at his Tiljala headquarters. Baba's Personal Assistant, Dada Keshavananda, was massaging Baba for a short time. Baba seemed very relaxed and rested. Then He said, "I have something on my mind. Please leave me for a little while."

A few minutes later Baba rang His bell and PA returned. Baba pointed to His chest and said, "Heart!" Two Margii doctors who lived in the jagrti came running and started taking all the necessary steps. However Baba stopped breathing and His heart stopped. There had been no pain. Finally the doctors had to declare that Baba was dead.

There were tears in my eyes the day you left
I could not stop myself that night

You looked me in the eyes and said,
"Come now, I am leaving your world, don't forget me."

I said, "When will you come? How many ages will pass?"
You said, "We will meet in love if you call."

—*Prabhat Samgiit, no. 2987*

Baba came into the world naturally and He left naturally. Baba always emphasized being natural and downplayed the supernatural, including His own supernatural abilities. Instead He stressed Ideology and Paramapurusa. One mistake, Baba said, that Krsna made, was to take credit for the Mahabrata (the great war that was said to establish dharma). By leaving His body the way He did and when He did, He avoided this mistake. Leaving at the beginning of at least a decade of unprecedented global crisis and catastrophy, He was allowing history to recognise the supremacy of Ideology over His physical presence.

> *"While in this physical body I am guiding you on the physico-psychic level. The energy I am infusing in the Mission is molecular. The speed of the Mssion will be enhanced after my physical departure. I will then guide you on the psycho-spiritual level and the Mission will move with more than atomic speed. "*
> —October 16, 1990

As the news of His death spread wholetimers and Margiis from all over the world rushed to Calcutta. When I arrived there was a long line of devotees waiting to see His body, which was enclosed in a glass case and preserved with ice. As I walked in I could see many expressions of pain and disbelief at the Lord's sudden departure. No one expected it, although with hindsight Baba gave some hints. For example, He told His niece Rani:

"You know, when a father leaves his family the children will have many problems, won't they?"

Rani replied, "Yes Baba."

Then He added, "But it will be allright."

> *"A dull brain cannot be a revolutionary. Hence one should be put in the most adverse and difficult circumstances and then left to come out of them by one's own stength. This will sharpen the brain and thinking capacity."*

Baba creates circumstances all the time for us which sharpen our minds like this. Baba leaving us has put all our dull minds in a position where we will have our thinking capacities sharpened from all the clash this has brought!

> *"Japakriya and dhyana should be practised with the ideation that one is serving Paramapurusa. This is internal service. If internal service is not rendered properly, true external service becomes impossible. Hence it is said 'Individual salvation is also a service to humanity.' External service purifies the mind, and with a pure mind one is more capable of rendering service to one's Ista. Every sadhaka should render both types of service."*

Three weeks before on Vijotsava, August 29th, Baba quoted the spiritual poet Kabir, "The world smiled when I cried but when I smiled the world cried." Baba explained that the poem means that at my birth when I came into this earth in pain and shock, I cried yet everyone was happy. When I left this world having completed my life's work, I smiled but the world cried.

In His last years, Baba was in such a hurry he did more even more work than usual. Five days previous to His passing, He personally initiated 79 avadhutas and avadhutikas, the largest number ever.

At His Mahaprayan we were allowed to walk around His body, do pranam and leave. Like everyone else, I had grieved considerably after learning of His death. However when I first looked at His body the grief vanished. As I gazed at His face, a strong image of Him appeared in my mind. Baba was full of joy which in turn filled me with joy. I realised what I was seeing was no longer Baba, merely a vehicle He once used to do worldly work. Now He had discarded it, having completed His physical work.

One month earlier in hospital Baba had said, "The future has come, the crimson dawn has already arrived. Just go on doing your duty. The work is already finished."

> *"When some people hesitate and doubt whether they can accomplish something, and if they start to work in that hesitant frame of mind, they can never accomplish that task. But if they plunge into action thinking of their goal with courage, imbued with spiritual inspiration, they are sure to be crowned with success."*

After realising my Baba was no longer in His body, I came to see His form two or three times more and each time I felt more strongly I was not seeing Baba. He told me internally that if I wanted to see Him I should go and do more sadhana. So I did.

The next day His form was cremated. Many thousands of devotees packed Tiljala's front compound to watch the cremation. A big six-pointed Pratik form had been built for the ceremony. During the ceremony a flock of pigeons flew over the crowd, circled directly above Baba's body and then settled on the nearby roof. It was as if they were making a final salute to their creator. Even Prakrti showed some tears in the form of rain for a few seconds. As Kimshuk, Baba's adopted son, lit the pyre, some crying could be heard from the crowd, but I felt nothing, feeling it had nothing to do with my Baba. Throughout the ceremony a *vanii* [spiritual message] Baba once gave in jail was repeated over and over again. It was appropriate.

If you want to see me, do my Mission because I am merged in my Mission. I am not this physical body, this physical body is not me. I am merged in your hearts and you are in mine. Only devotion can demand my physical presence.

During those days leading up to the cremation I heard from so many devotees the same conclusion, "Baba has not died—only His physical from has gone." Also everyone from the General Secretary down, emphasized the importance of sadhana as the means to keep in touch with Him.

> *"Don't be concerned with your individual problems. Be prepared to carry your own burden and be prepared to carry the burden of others. Then alone you are brave."*

In Tantra it is said that when Guru leaves His physical form, His astral and spiritual forms remain to guide His devotees. Baba also once said:

In the past I helped sadhakas to obtain the Blissful state, I am helping sadhakas at present, and I shall help also in the future through other means, even when I shall not remain physically.

Also:

The physical from is not the Guru but the entity behind this physical form is the Guru. Therefore Brahma alone is the Guru.

It is also said that when Sadguru takes physical form, He withholds a lot of His sweetness and vibration. However when He leaves He removes all restraints, therefore spiritual practices become even more sweet and blissful after He has gone. So to get His darshan and guidance from the higher subtle levels, and also to enjoy His full force, sadhana is of paramount importance.

Sadhana is also important for understanding His ideology and for fulfilling His mission. Regarding ideology He said, "Those who love my ideology love me. But those who say they love me but don't love my ideology, I doubt whether they really love me."

*"Never do anything for others for personal purpose.
Do everything for the Ideology."*

The feeling after the cremation was "For Baba alone we must establish His mission. We must do more sadhana and remain ever united." All over the globe devotees were taking an oath which Baba had recently asked wholetimers and Margiis to take.

All my energy, all my mind, all my thoughts and all my deeds are to be goaded unto the path of collective elevation of human society, without neglecting other living and inanimate entities, right from this moment to the last moment of my living on this earth.

Baba came, He loved, guided and inspired, then He left. To me the most important thing He left us was not just the amazing spiritual sciences, Prout and Microvita, Neo-humanist philosophy and the huge and comprehensive social service organisations, the over three hundred books covering all possible subjects, 5018 Prabhat Samgiit, not to speak of in His last year, Gurukula, Gurusakasha and the concept of transmutation of psychic pabula... as great as these are, the greatest thing is His personal example of how we are to live in the world. Whether we are a sannyasi or family person, a sadhaka or organisational activist or revolutionary, Baba left a perfect example. He encapsulated the exemplary life in *bhavisca* mantra which He once gave to some Margiis and non-Margiis to follow as a guide. It means "Love of God, modesty, self-restraint and good conduct."

> *"Those with spiritual lethargy have time for all other actions, but for spiritual practice there seems to be no time. They say, 'It's already late today, I'll do a short meditation right now, and devote more time to sadhana tomorrow. They sit attentively inside the cinema hall, but in Dharma Sadhana they feel sleepy."*

Of course for those very fortunate ones who have personal experiences of His physical form, He has left a sweet memory which will remain with them until their last breath if not longer. Even those who have not experienced Him physically, the stories told of such divine experiences will be a source of inspiration for future generations and centuries to come.

Nothing has changed spiritually. Baba always said He was to be found internally, not in His external form, He often said, "I am with you." Now there is no option but to go deep within to experience Him. Bhagavan is here as ever, waiting for us to come to Him, to sit in His loving lap and enjoy His real darshan.

> *"In sadhana one should remember two essential factors: constant awareness of one's goal, and persistent endeavour to attain that goal."*

The memories and stories of His visit to 20th century planet Earth will live on but still much remains a mystery, for He is beyond words and the mind. As Baba Himself said, "I was a mystery, I am a mystery, I will always remain a mystery." But what a sweet and loving mystery Gurudeva was and will always be.

Na Gururadhikam, Na Gururadhikam, Na Gururadhikam
Shivashasanta Ha, Shivashatsanta Ha, Shivashatsanta Ha

There is nothing higher than the Guru,
There is nothing higher than the Guru,
There is nothing higher than the Guru,
This is the word of Shiva,
This is the word of Shiva,
This is the word of Shiva

"Where there is Dharma, there is Ishta,
where there is Ishta there is Victory!"

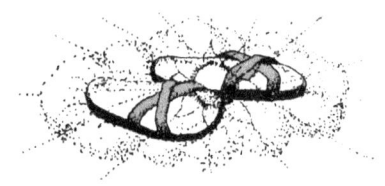

Appendix 1: Secrets of Spirituality

Sadhana is the vital link between Bhagavan and His devotee. If the link is not strong, then it will be difficult to come close to Him.

Baba gave these following instructions on some important aspects of sadhana, to His long-time devotee, Nagina. The following information in this chapter is taken from Nagina's writings.

I inquired of Baba, "Baba, can one fall even after attaining the Savikalpa and Nirvikalpa stage?"

Baba replied in the affirmative.

I again inquired as to why and how it happened.

Baba replied, "If a sadhaka does sadhana with great intensity, regularity and for long hours, he attains Savikalpa and Nirvikalpa soon. But the burden of his samskaras will still remain.

"If his samskaras are good, there is nothing to worry about. But it is also possible that in the coming times the bundle of samskaras unfolding in him are not good. In such circumstances, it is in the interest of the welfare of the sadhaka that he keeps close contact with the Guru, otherwise there is the fear of fall."

I inquired as to how. Baba kindly further explained and said, "When samskaras are not good, they are bound to reveal their effect and shape and will disturb the sadhaka. But if the sadhaka is in contact with the Guru, the Guru, by His grace, makes the sadhaka exhaust these samskaras in a controlled manner.

"It may be necessary to give greater self confidence or patience to the sadhaka in such times so that he may bear the change in the normal way and may not deviate from the path. But, this is possible only when the sadhaka is in contact with the Guru. But even after attaining the goal of sadhana, bad samskaras may be left over and due to their pressure his contact with the Guru may have been severed. In that event, these samskaras will move the sadhaka towards a fall. Without the Guru's grace, all the efforts of such a sadhaka are in vain and his fall is inevitable. Therefore, Guru kindly withdraws the state of Nirvikalpa and Savikdpa from him before his fall so that the coming generations on the spiritual path may not be confused by his high spiritual attainments and low mental states."

Baba also pointed out that to withdraw the Nirvikalpa from the Sadhaka, the Guru comes in the Savikalpa stage. This is a very painful task, yet it has to be performed....

Guru Puja

For many days, I was keen to enquire about the process and the meaning of Guru Puja....

Baba told me that Guru Puja has three names: *Guru Puja, Varnaghyadan* and *Nimitahar*. First, there are three couplets in the Guru Puja mantra. You recite them audibly and every time you offer flowers, mentally or physically, to the Guru. This is Guru Puja.

Second, at the end of the last couplet, you offer flowers of your chosen color to the Guru. This is also either mental or in reality. This process is varnaghyadan. *Varna* means color and every tendency or propensity of the mental world has its own color. Whatever vritti dominates you at a given moment, is the color you are attracted to.

Therefore, it is prescribed to offer the flower of your chosen color. During Guru Puja, naturally the color will come to your mind, which is your most dominant propensity. By offering that color to the Guru, you will be free of that vritti or propensity.

Third is *Nimitahar*. The color and form that you offer to the Guru is His staple and regular food. These propensities are obstacles in the path of the sadhaka and when they are offered at the feet of the Guru, the Guru very kindly accepts them. Therefore, you have to do Guru Puja and Varnaghyadan regularly both morning and evening. By omitting this, you starve the Guru. But, the sadhaka has to be extremely careful at the time of Guru Puja and Varnaghyadan lest a mistake should not be in the process, otherwise Guru may not accept the offered propensity. Nimitahar is entirely at the sweet will of the Guru—He may or He may not accept.

I asked Baba whether '*Varnaghyadan*' is the surest way for sadhakas to be free of their propensities. Baba replied in the affirmative saying that by doing it along with sadhana, the speed of sadhana is accelerated.

"Do you know why? Do you know why Guru Puja is done at the end of sadhana?" Baba asked.

I replied that I did not know.

Baba pointed out that the propensities which disturbed the concentration of your mind at the time of doing sadhana and have disturbed your dhyana, are fresh in your mind at the end of your sadhana and so should be offered to the Guru at this time. By following this practice regularly, a sadhaka is cleansed of those propensities. There are some people whose minds fail to imagine or visualise the correct colors. They should purchase papers of all the seven colors and they should keep the pieces with them so that they may select one of them for the offering of the flower.

The Perfect Environment

That day Baba was extremely kind and was pointing out some things about sadhana which are very useful for the entire sadhaka community. I have taken the liberty to write them down here. They appear very simple but are full of great significance and value.

Baba said that a sadhaka should convert their house and body into a temple. The house will become a temple only when there are constant vibrations of sadhana in its environment. Such an environment is only possible when all the residents of that house perform sadhana every day with sincerity and devotion. This is how a house can be made into a temple.

By following the eightfold path of sadhana of Astaunga Yoga with devotion, faith and regularity, this body is also converted into a temple. Astaunga Yoga includes yama and niyama (morality), asanas, pranayama (breath control), pratyahara (withdrawal), dharana (concentration), dhyana (deep meditation) and samadhi.

"If the gap between moralism and universalism is to be conquered, then spiritual sadhana is a must. They [Neo-humanists], therefore, must practice austere sadhana. Their philosophy of life will be 'morality is the base, sadhana is the means and Life Divine is the Goal"

Baba further pointed out that every sadhaka should select a secluded spot in their house where they perform sadhana morning and evening. They should also choose an *asan* ("seat" such as a mat or blanket) for sadhana which will not be used for other purposes or by other people. Then they should also fix a regular time for sadhana. By following these instructions, sadhana will always be of good quality.

As for the *asan*, either tiger skin or deer skin or a blanket, a mat or a 'dori' will do. But one must always ensure that the asan should be a non-conductor of heat otherwise the energy gained by sadhana will not be preserved as the earth is a bad conductor of heat. [Baba has said that a black wool blanket is perfect for asan.]

Baba simplified the matter further by explaining that due to fixing, time, place and 'asan', the mind becomes familiar with that environment and will be able to concentrate easily. Its the same as when your sleeping place and time are fixed so that you fall asleep as soon as you lie there. But if the place is changed, or the bedding is not yours, or has been changed, and the time is also not of your choice, it will take time to fall asleep. The same is applicable to sadhana also.

Baba further pointed out that sadhana should always be done in a peaceful and pleasant mood. One should not do it when one is angry or dejected. In such a situation, all efforts to concentrate the mind will be wasted.

> *"In the culture of knowledge one remains where one was. In ... karma one remains preoccupied with hundreds of actions. If there is no Bhakti, one will never come in the proximity of Paramapurusa."*

You should sit in the lotus posture at the time of sadhana. The lotus posture keeps one in a pleasant temper. You will find that one who is accustomed to doing the lotus posture will always be of an amicable temper.

Do not touch anything like water up to half an hour after sadhana. This will enable the energy created by sadhana not to pass away in that medium.

If due to some reason, the mind does not concentrate on some days, then give more time to the *shuddhis*. This will improve concentration.

That day Baba was bent upon explaining to me—of dull intellect—the specialities of sadhana. Baba knew that my mind was fond of logic and therefore, he was explaining the logic behind most of the processes of sadhana.

In this context, Baba asked, "How will you know that the mantra given to you is correct and proper?"

I pleaded ignorance and said that I only know how to repeat it in the given manner.

Baba said, "No, you should know whether you have the right mantra or not. You should know the criteria for this. If there is growth in the situation and circumstances under which you took initiation, then that mantra is correct.

"Suppose you took initiation in happy circumstances, then the happiness should grow and if you received initiation when the circumstances were painful, then their intensity should grow. This is the test of a correct mantra. The I'sta Mantra acts like fire for the accumulated heap of your samskaras which can be compared to gun powder. Therefore, the situation which was there at the time of initiation will aggravate.

"In extremes of either happiness or pain there is a possibility of deviation from the path of sadhana. Therefore, in extremes situations if you keep contact with the Guru, you will get extra mental strength to bear the circumstances."

In this regard, I have a special experience that the Guru's darshan also aggravates samskaras, particularly the painful ones. They become explosive and the disciple begins to writhe with pain under their painful pressure. At times, the disciple, even the senior disciples find themselves besieged with danger and difficulties. The impending adversities begin to disturb their mental equilibrium.

But this is also the time of test for their courage and patience. If they courageously and patiently continue to take the support of the Guru and remain steadfast in their devotion and Guru darshan, then certainly Guru will give them the extra mental strength to bear the adversity.

> *"Your ista mantra is your most cherished object."*

I'sta Mantra
Baba said about the I'sta mantra:
"The sadhaka should constantly do the *japa* [internal repetition] of I'sta mantra. The practice of japa with the breath should be advanced to such an extent that the body may be busy in any activity, but the mind will continue to repeat the I'sta mantra within every breath.

"When you are doing something, the eyes should remain open. Suppose you are going somewhere on foot or on a bicycle or in a car which you are driving yourself. If at that time you do the japa of I'sta Mantra with closed eyes, there may be an accident. Therefore, while working, eyes will remain open and japa will continue with the breathing."

I asked, "Baba, when one walks or cycles, the breath becomes irregular and therefore there is a disturbance in the japa, also.

Baba said, "In that situation adjust the breath with the movement of right and left foot and then do the japa. This will protect the rhythm of the japa."

One who is established in the practice of the I'sta Mantra will die at his or her own wish only–they will never die an accidental death. There is nothing like an accident, in the sense that every event is an incident. Where people fail to locate the cause behind an event, they call it an accident.

> *"The only true progress for human beings is spiritual progress. The wise will, therefore, concern themselves only with the spiritual sphere. The only concern with the physical and intellectual spheres will be adjusting the base on which spiritual progress will thrive."*

Baba pointed out that the mind has three stages or layers: conscious, subconscious and unconscious. At the time of doing sadhana, you are hitting the conscious mind. In this process the layer of the conscious mind becomes subtle. The effect of this hitting of the mantra goes to the subconscious mind. In this condition, the sadhaka starts hearing or seeing wonderful experiences and he or she starts feeling some kind of peace in his or her mind. By further regular practice of I'sta mantra, the subconscious level also starts getting subtler, and the striking of the mantra starts affecting the unconscious mind. The sadhaka then starts knowing the events of the future. Gradually, as one starts getting established in Iishvara Pranidhana, one becomes omniscient.

> *"The actual idea in your mind should be that Parama Purusa has kept a close watch over you in the past, is keeping a close watch over you now, and will keep a close watch over you in the future. Under no circumstances are you alone or neglected. As long as you remember that Paramapurusa is watching, no power in this universe can oppose or harm you. Moreover, each and every entity from the Supreme Creator of the Universe to a single blade of grass, will cooperate fully with you."*

Gurusakash

Baba recommends this practice for all sadhakas. Performed sincerely it becomes the guiding force for all action in the day. He has said that every sadhaka should remember the Guru in the *guru cakra* immediately upon waking:

...sitting in the posture of *Siddhasana* or any other convenient *asana*, on the same blanket, leather, seat or bed as they had used for sleeping, immediately after waking up and before doing any other work or before having any other thought, even before performing their morning duties or any other task. This will be a high category of gurusakash. If it cannot always be done after waking up, it is particularly essential to remember the Guru in the morning after sleep. If this is done they will meet with success in each and every subtle and spiritual task that they perform in the course of the whole day. It is said:

Pra'tah shirasi shukle'abje dvinetram' dvibhujam' gurum'
Bara'bhayakrtahastam' smarattam' na'mapu'rvakam

'Early in the morning one should meditate on the Guru in Vara'bhaya Mudra with two hands and two eyes seated on a white lotus in guru cakra, and address Him with your most loving and affectionate epithet.' "

"Make your existence great by dint of your extraordinary action. Your life will become more and more meaningful if you do more and more work and more and more meditation."

Appendix 2: Perfecting Sadhana

The following is an article I wrote for *Pranam* magazine around 1988. It is a review of some of the important points that help when you want to deepen your sadhana. I collected this information from a number of acharyas during different visits to India over the years.

A Good Stomach
   The stomach should be empty and bowels clear before sadhana. Generally the digestive tract should be free from discomfort as it will irritate the mind and disturb sadhana. Therefore, proper food is very important. Not only should food be sentient, but it should be easily digestible, particularly at night.
   Ideally the evening meal should consist of fruit and milk and should be eaten before eight pm, and not later than 9:00. The later the meal, the lighter and smaller (in quantity) should be the food eaten. Heavy meals, especially late at night, lead to a tamasic sleep and similar sadhana in the morning.
   Sadhakas over the age of 29 should avoid sugar. At the least, it should be restricted to a minimum as it is bad for the nerves and brain, and therefore sadhana.

One of Shiva's seven secrets for spiritual success is balanced and nutritious food. Never underestimate its importance for sadhana.

Satsaunga

According to Tantra, good company or *satsanga* leads to liberation and bad company leads to bondage or degeneration. The serious sadhaka has to be very careful about the company they keep. The attitude should be to desire or prefer only sentient or spiritual company, avoiding as far as possible crude and even rajasik people.

Rajasic people are those whose nature tends towards, among other things, talkativeness, gossiping, criticising and groupism. These activities are very harmful to the serious sadhaka and must be avoided. What is thought, said and heard comes up in sadhana and so if these mental impressions are negative or vain, your sadhana will also take on these qualities.

Satsanga is of two kinds: external (company with other sadhakas) and internal (keeping company with Parama Purusa). Of the two, internal satsaunga is the best. The more one experiences Baba, the more one prefers internal satsanga and will desire less the company of others. This has nothing to do with becoming antisocial. When one falls in love the natural inclination is to want to be alone with one's beloved. Similarly the more one experiences Baba's love, the more one wants to be only with only Baba. Being alone and in quiet lonely places enables one's full attention to be directed inwards toward His love. Love is a very private, personal affair and is often difficult to share with others.

Guru and Ista Mantras

We must cultivate the habit of constant use of Guru and Ista mantras. Not only should we use Guru Mantra at the compulsory times— before eating, sleeping, sadhana and bath—but before all activities. If you have difficulty following the previous point (satsaunga) above because of a tendency towards talkativeness, try using Guru mantra before speaking and the problem will be solved! Ista mantra should be repeated continuously regardless of what you are doing. If it is practiced all day then you will hear it even in dreams, and when you awake, there it will be!

To sit for sadhana and then afterwards forget all about the goal of life represented by these two mantras makes sadhana much less meaningful. Work and service develop vainty if there is no ideation and working with vanity isn't real service. Therefore, this point is extremely important. Quality sadhana makes this ideation much easier to develop, however, a conscious effort still has to be made to use the mantras.

The capacity to withdraw the mind back to your ideation when it has been distracted or forgotten is crucial here. Often the mind will resist because of its attachment to a conversation or to work, for example. However, the sadhaka must learn to overcome this weakness. We must be able to redirect the mind back to Baba the moment we realise that our ideation on Him is lost. This capacity to withdraw the mind back to our ideation greatly affects our capacity for sadhana.

Due to our lifestyle, our work and our samskaras, we may or may not be able to keep good company all the time. However, we can all repeat our Ista and Guru mantras all the time and enjoy His internal company.

Proper Shuddhis

If you are having difficulty in sadhana, then it is quite likely that you are not doing the shuddhis properly (the system for withdrawal of the mind before sadhana.) Therefore, if for example, you have one hour for sadhana, 45 minutes should be devoted to the shuddhis and 15 minutes to mantra or dhyana. If the shuddhis are done properly then ideation will become very strong. Indeed, it is said that if the shuddhis are done properly then the mantra need be repeated only once with ideation and one will experience samadhi.

However, if after doing the shuddhis properly there is still no bliss, it means there is no devotion. If so, 45 minutes should be spent on kiirtan, ten minutes on shuddhis and five minutes on mantra.

> *"The actual idea in your mind should be that Parama Purusa has kept a close watch over you in the past, is keeping a close watch over you now, and will keep a close watch over you in the future. Under no circumstances are you alone or neglected. As long as you remember that Paramapurusa is watching, no power in this universe can oppose or harm you. Moreover, each and every entity from the Supreme Creator of the Universe to a single blade of grass, will cooperate fully with you."*

Consistency

We must be consistent in the amount of sadhana we do daily. Set a minimum amount of time and stick to it. One Dada suggested we should do no less than one hour every time we sit for sadhana, while another said to do at least four hours each day. I prefer the latter because most of it can be done in the morning (providing you get up early) while noon and evening sadhanas are often shortened or neglected because of work or family commitments.

However you decide to do it, be consistent! Any spiritual flow gained by sadhana will be lost if this consistency is not maintained. In the long run, nothing will be achieved spiritually. Determination and perseverance is needed to be consistent in sadhana. If due to an exceptional work load such as emergency relief work, sadhana is reduced, then as soon as circumstances return to normal, do twice as much sadhana for as long as you didn't practice the regular minimum amount. Remember, nothing, great can be achieved without the strength of mind (and ideation) gained from proper sadhana.

Straight Back

A straight back is very, very important for sadhana. Whatever can be achieved with a curved back, one thousand times more can be achieved with a straight back. While I was doing long sadhana in prison, I noticed that the only time I felt intense love and bliss was when my back was very straight. If my back was not straight, I could do sadhana for hours but nothing would happen.

Kula kundalinii, or the serpentine spiritual force, travels up the spine sending the sadhaka deeper into sadhana and bliss. The straighter the spine, the easier it is for the kundalinii to rise. Often during good sadhana, the kundalini "jumps" causing the back to jump and become very stiff and straight. This position is the ideal posture for sadhana.

Proper Use of Energy

Energy is one, but it can be expressed in the physical, mental or emotional and spiritual spheres. Energy is limited and to put too much energy into one form of expression will reduce the desire and capacity for expression in other areas. People who do a lot of sport or study, for example, will not have much energy for spiritual practices. Likewise one who does a lot of sadhana will not feel much attraction for physical or intellectual expression. Ideally, there should be a balance between the three, or perhaps, as some sadhakas say, a bias towards or emphasis on, spiritual expression.

Conservation of energy important because spiritual development requires a huge effort. Therefore, our energy (and time) should not be wasted in useless thought, speech and action. Always use your energy with restraint and ideation. Especially when you are outside family life, avoid physical contact with other people as much as possible. It is draining and disruptive to ideation. The exception is in service to others such ascaring for children or nursing the sick or when you are receiving service such as when youare being treated for an illness. Married people can have more physical contact, however, sex should be kept to a minimum: ideally no more than four times each month. However sexual suppression is also harmful, so its important to keep a balanced approach.

Ideally, sadhana should be done alone or at least five feet from another person, except with you married partner or children. Of course Dharmacakra is also an exception. Avoid doing sadhana in a room where someone is sleeping or talking. Other people's vibrations also can disrupt sadhana.

Bandhu Prabhat Samgiita

From a devotional and spiritual perspective, we should learn those Prabhat Samgiita which express a very close relationship with Baba as represented in the concept of *"bandhu"* (the very closest friend). These are the songs which describe great closeness, love and affection or, alternatively, the pain and clash we experience when we feel distant from Him. We can choose an appropriate song according to our mood each day. Either type of song will bring love and bliss.

On the point of lyrics, it is very important to know not only the line by line meaning, but also the word for word meaning, just like the mantras of Third Lesson. Singing Prabhat Samgiita without knowing its meaning, especially the inner meaning, is far less effective.

Maximum Dhyana

Do as much dhyana (Sixth Lesson) as you can. Don't limit it to regular sadhana times. You can practice dhyana while you are sitting in the bus or the car, or while waiting for someone. Whenever there is a spare moment, do some dhyana! Ultimately life has to become one long dhyana, a loving service to Baba.

There are two important points to remember for dhyana:

First, there must be intense love for Baba. As He said, we should feel, "I love my Lord, I love Him. My love knows no barriers ... " Dhyana cannot be done without feeling this intense, close love for Him.

The second point is that we must feel that He is watching us doing the sadhana. Baba is the subject and we are the object. Baba explained:

> During meditation you should think that the entity on whom you are meditating is looking at you as His object. He is not your object. He sees whatever you are doing. This should be the psychology ... He is not your object, you are His object. (*Ananda Vacanamrtam*, Part VI)

Not only should we feel Ba'ba' watching us in dhyana, but during all of our sadhana and daily ideation. If you have ever experienced Baba looking at you, in life or dream, then carry that feeling in sadhana—it's very powerful.

Our capacity to follow those two points will greatly determine our capacity to do dhyana.

To make dhyana a "living practice" it is important to not only ideate on Ista and Guru mantras, but also to think as much as possible about Baba all of the time. In whatever way you can, remember Him. It does not matter which way, as long as He is constantly in your mind.

Miscellaneous Points
- Choose a sadhana mat or blanket and use it for nothing but sadhana. Ideally, choose one room or small area which is also used exculsively for sadhana. This will create a conducive atmosphere for deep spiritual ideation.

• While doing sadhana, you may change your leg position according to what is comfortable, but always keep your eyes closed. If you feel tired, or find yourself rocking, sleeping or slumping during sadhana, take a half bath and then resume your sadhana. It will refresh you and, in the case a long sadhana, it will give you a chance to stretch your legs as well. But during such a break, do not talk with anyone. Of course, the longer you can go without a break the better (providing you are not sleeping).

• Do sadhana at regular times. Late sadhana generally means late meals and work which, in turn, mean less sadhana and work. This is where consistency and determination come in. Also, when you are not observing satsaunga and are engaged in too much chatter or pointless action , then sadhana times get delayed more and more. In the end, neither sadhana or work is performed properly. Proper use of energy should be applied here, too.

• Svadhyaya is important for sadhana. *Subhasiita Samgraha* or *Ananda Vacanamrtam* should be read daily. Chapter 3 and the last five chapters of *Namami Krsnasundarum* give a very deep insight into spiritual devotion and the ideal ideation to have for Baba, particularly in dhyana.

• Always try to keep your body cool because sadhana produces a lot of heat. Avoid a lot of direct hot sun, unless your in a cool climate. Don't do sadhana in the hot sun and even when the sun is not hot, don't face the sun, do sadhana with your back to it.

• Do sadhana when your left nostril is open. If it is not, do more kiirtan or lie on your right side until it is open.

• Asanas give health, concentration, restraint and a calm temperament. Do them regularly, slowly and with ideation, holding them for the prescribed time. Also pranayama (Fourth Lesson) and Guru Puja should be done slowly with ideation and not be not rushed. When these are rushed it is almost as bad as not doing them at all.

• Sleeping during the day, unless you are sick, is tamasik and should be avoided. The deepest sleep is normally between 10:00 pm and midnight. Arise before 5:00 am for Paincajanya is an extremely beneficial and important practice.

All these points are aids to perfecting sadhana. As with all aspects of the 16 points, all that is needed to follow them is sincerity and faith. Don't be concerned that some points seem so difficult. With sincerity and regular sadhana, eventually all the points will become achievable.

www.ingramcontent.com/pod-product-compliance
Lightning Source LLC
Chambersburg PA
CBHW070626300426
44113CB00010B/1676